Essays from the Nick of Time

Also by Mark Slouka

Fiction
The Visible World
God's Fool
Lost Lake

Nonfiction
War of the Worlds

Essays from the Nick of Time

Reflections and Refutations

Mark Slouka

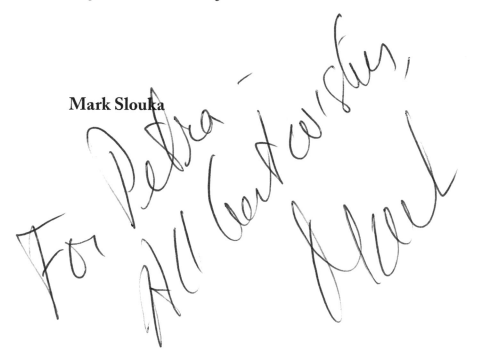

GRAYWOLF PRESS

"Hitler's Couch," "Arrow and Wound," "Eclogue," "Listening for Silence," "Blood on the Tracks," "Quitting the Paint Factory," "One Year Later," "Democracy and Deference," and "Dehumanized" were first published in *Harper's Magazine*. "Hitler's Couch," "Listening for Silence," and "Arrow and Wound" were also published in *Best American Essays 1999, 2000*, and *2003*, respectively. "Speak, Video" was first published in the *Georgia Review*. "Historical Vertigo" was first published in *AGNI*.

This publication is made possible by funding provided in part by a grant from the Minnesota State Arts Board, through an appropriation by the Minnesota State Legislature, a grant from the National Endowment for the Arts, and private funders. Significant support has also been provided by Target; the McKnight Foundation; and other generous contributions from foundations, corporations, and individuals. To these organizations and individuals we offer our heartfelt thanks.

NATIONAL ENDOWMENT FOR THE ARTS

MINNESOTA STATE ARTS BOARD

WELLS FARGO

TARGET.

Published by Graywolf Press
250 Third Avenue North, Suite 600
Minneapolis, Minnesota 55401

All rights reserved.

www.graywolfpress.org

Published in the United States of America

ISBN 978-1-55597-571-5

2 4 6 8 9 7 5 3 1
First Graywolf Printing, 2010

Library of Congress Control Number: 2010922924

Cover design: Kimberly Glyder Design

Cover art: Tina Mion, *It was obvious upon seeing Joan of Arc even God couldn't save her.*

For my parents,
who taught me that skepticism is just a deeper form of reverence,
and anger and wonder its purest expressions.

And for Leslie, Zack, and Maya,
who daily make me grateful to be here
to wrestle with and marvel at the world for a while.

I have been anxious to improve the nick of time . . . ;
to stand on the meeting of two eternities, the past and future,
which is precisely the present moment; to toe that line.
—THOREAU

Contents

Introduction

There may be someone even less suited to introducing a writer's work than the author himself—a well-meaning relative, perhaps, or a lover with a grudge—but I doubt it. We're the wrong people for the job; we approach demolition with a scalpel, surgery with a five-foot crowbar and a mallet. Despite this fact, most of us, unless we've grown sufficiently famous to affect disinterest convincingly, or retreated into enigmatic seclusion, will rise to the editor's suggestion that we "say a few words" like gullible trout to a plastic cricket. It seems harmless, even interesting. It's not.

There are many reasons for this, some obvious, most hidden in plain view. I've listed a few here as a kind of public service, a detour around the tar pit in which I flounder.

1. We're Bound to Disappoint

A decade ago, before the gene for reclusiveness that I carry began to assert itself, I attended a *Harper's Magazine* dinner at which I found myself seated at a very long, very wide table, stranded between people engaged in lively conversations. There was nothing to do but eavesdrop and eat. At some point, an attractive young woman directly across from me noticed my plight. "Who are you?" she called, with admirable directness. I told her. "Oh, *you're* Mark Slouka,"

she said. I smiled; indeed I was. "You know, it's funny, but
I thought you'd look different," she said. My ego began to
hiss quietly. "How so?" I asked. "I don't know," she said, "I
thought you'd be sort of dark and brooding and marked by
tragedy."

What would I have given then for Paul Auster's eyes,
or even Kafka's? For a scar or a cape. Ignore the ill-fitting
tie and the Vladimir Putin hairline, I wanted to say; trust
me, inside I'm as dark and brooding as they come. I went
home, brooded. Perhaps the dark jacket next time? The following day I mentioned the incident at home and paid the
predictable price: Dad was dark and brooding and marked
by acne, pale and shallow and . . . but you get the idea. Our
clan, on the whole, is not given to coddling.

The anecdotal point? The words are who we are. They are
our introduction. And our conclusion. To introduce them,
therefore, is largely redundant, and because we sense this,
because we feel we need something *more,* we rush backstage
and drag our other self, like a shy director to a curtain call,
into the limelight. Like most acts of desperation, it's a bad
idea. Best to let the curtain (or the cover) close.

2. We Know Too Much

Generally speaking, writers who have been at it for a while,
and who are any good at it, suffer from an acute kind of
self-knowledge. The unexamined life is not a risk for them.
They've spent years studying themselves, parsing themselves; they're familiar with every tic and foible. Their own
worst inclinations—toward pomposity, toward sentimentality, toward cuteness or tripe—are old, familiar adversaries;
they've wrestled with them for years. And because of this,
because they know every grip and feint, writers become
very good at running defense, at masking or deflecting or,

if necessary, shaping what is potentially embarrassing into a strength, an asset.

In short, they lack the ignorance to sum themselves well. The conversation—this lifelong disarticulation of the self—is ongoing; they resume it every time they sit down at their desks. How can they label the thing when it won't stay on the slide; when it keeps growing out, branching; when every definitive statement ("My work is this," "What I was after here was this") immediately feels false, straining to grow a comma and a conjunction? How can they even begin without ignoring the strange, shifting country of human motivation with its thickets of regret, its clever labyrinths of self-justification and denial, its frozen meadows of nonnegotiable love?

And so they—we—lie; we summarize, we get cute. Because it wouldn't do to say that we have no idea, really, why we wrote something, what particular force forced our hand, we *say* we do. Because we're not sure what it is that compels us, like planets on a fixed orbit, to revisit the same places, to be drawn by the same sun that drew us ten years ago, or twenty, we pretend. We affect certainty; our hindsight vision is raptor-sharp. All in all, it's not so hard to pull off: a general air of competence and self-control, a few writerly aphorisms, a touch of arrogance tempered by a julienne of whimsy or wit, and the thing is done. Everyone is satisfied; the check—a small one—arrives in the mail.

3. Time Disassembles

However difficult it may be to introduce a single work, introducing a collection of pieces written over a period of years is infinitely more so. Time—never mind its other sins—complicates things. Everything, actually. To run with my astronomy analogy for a moment, though the general path of our interests may remain constant, our understanding of the places we visit will change with age, in large part because the bodies we pass will have moved in their own right, forcing new perspectives.

Like frost—to ground the metaphor—time forces things, exposes failures of understanding or compassion, takes what might otherwise appear to be whole and reveals the fissures, the accidents, the glue lines. Given enough years, everything—our lives, our work—can begin to look cobbled, a bit of this, a bit of that, "because it seemed like a good idea at the time." Which is okay, maybe. Madness, like Ahab's, runs on iron rails to its fixed goal; the rest of us make it up as we go along. We shift, we adapt, then deny it, strenuously. We're a bit of a mess. We cling passionately to certain ways and means of being long after they've outlived their time; we embrace constancy as though it were always a virtue and never a sin.

A collection written over fifteen or twenty years, unless it be tightly restricted by subject, or trapped in the academic corral, is a bumpy thing, marked by scars and age spots, by contradictions and old refrains and stubborn retrenchments. Like the human being behind it, it will return to the same loves and gripes, essaying to find a way in. It will try different approaches, lenses, voices; laugh when laughing is possible, rage when rage is right. You can force a narrative onto it (after all, we do it to our lives all the time), slap a title on and cinch it tight, but the words, like the living, will escape every time.

An introduction, if it is anything, is an act of retrospection, and what could be more given to misreading than retrospection? Fifteen years ago, when I wrote the first of these essays, I was not yet thirty-six; my daughter was a toddler, my son barely four. I was in love with the same woman I'm in love with now—one constancy I don't regret. I'd like to think I was more foolish then, but that would be presuming too much. Periodically along the way, some curiosity, some unresolved thing, presented itself and I followed it. Other times, some turn-of-the-millennium irritation crawled across my desk, and I smacked it. E. B. White once wrote of Thoreau that he was trapped between wanting to celebrate the world, and wanting to fix it. That's a rack I recognize.

For a time I thought my fiction could allow me to do the first, my essays the second; that I could segregate the two. I was wrong. Though the work of fixing is anathema to fiction (except in the deepest, most abstract, most essential sense), my essays clearly do both. Or try. In fact, the longer I think about it, the less certain I am that the distinction between celebrating and fixing is useful. The most unabashedly political pieces here (those trained, often as not, on the second Bush administration, now happily receding in the rearview mirror) are celebrating something, something I believe needs defending, while the most meditative, by exploring the reflexiveness of memory, say, or the creative force of history, by celebrating, in other words, the sheer complexity of being alive in the world, can be seen as an attempt to fix our vision, which seems stuck, at times, on the simplistic and the trivial.

And so, fifteen years' worth of meditations and arguments and borderline polemics, some relatively small-bore, others admittedly after bigger, more enduring game. I can't sum them. Are they opinionated? Of course. Timidity belongs to other lines of work, not ours. Am I concerned that their occasional out of sync-ness with the times will cost me? Not a bit. Writers—unlike network anchorpersons or presidential speechwriters—are paid to stand outside the current and say what they see, and the readers worth having are those who appreciate the stance and the product.

For better or worse, I've resisted the temptation to tinker, to temper, to correct the too-sweeping generalization in light of future events. I've rebuffed my own maturity, perhaps because I don't entirely trust it. Similarly, though our history-in-the-microwave momentum has given one or two of these essays a slightly dated cast, I've allowed this layer of verdigris to remain, first, because the pace of change in our day, driven less by actual human needs than by the rational absurdities of the market, is one of my subjects, and second, because I believe that the din of apparent change can mask the fact that the new boss, like the new app, ain't, really. The name on the White House mailbox is less important than the American people's stance toward power; the fact that today's smartphone will be tomorrow's 8-track tape is less interesting than our touching faith in (make that "dazed infatuation with") all things technological. So the references to "Dubya" and video-cassettes stay.

What are these essays about? They're about the intersection of memory and history and fiction, because that is where I live as a writer. They're about America, because America is where I've spent the majority of my years. They're about how we work and how we remember and how we make sense (or not) of the things that happen to us. A number, I see, are about the losses exacted by what we've been trained to call progress, even when it's not. They are, like the essays of those I admire most, my attempts to get at what matters, or what I thought mattered at the time that I wrote them.

While I can't say much about them that they don't already say for themselves, I can say this: the essay form has allowed me to grapple with our world in all its atrociousness and beauty. It's been an outlet for speculation, a medium for wonder, a safety valve for emotion—for rage, let's say. At times it's conferred the illusion that we are not utterly helpless in the face of our species' routine depredations. And for this I am grateful.

REFLECTIONS

Hitler's Couch

1998

This was the Angel of History! We felt its
wings flutter through the room.
—SCHWERIN VON KROSIGK

I

If Stephen Dedalus, that fearful Jesuit, was right, if history, in the century of Bergen-Belsen and Nanking and Democratic Kampuchea, is a nightmare from which we are all—even the most effectively narcotized among us—trying to awake, how then do we explain the dream that foreshadows the event, the actual nightmare that precedes the waking one?

When he was eight years old, my father was visited by a nightmare so powerful that half a century later the mere retelling of it would stipple his skin with gooseflesh and lift the hair on the back of his arms. He himself would wonder at his own bristling body, the shameless atavism of fear. "Look at this," he'd say when I was young, shoving one big arm across the table. "It never fails." And seeing the coarse, familiar fur rise as if by some conjurer's trick to the memory of a dream decades gone, I'd know that the immaterial world was a force to be reckoned with.

In the dream (although nothing translates as badly as dreams—
no grief, no scent, no earthly grammar), my eight-year-old father
hurries, clockwise, down a white spiral staircase. The stairwell
has no windows, no central shaft; its sides are as smooth as a
chambered nautilus. Just ahead, the left-hand wall continuously
extends itself, emerging out of the seam.

He stops, suddenly aware of a sound coming from far below.
He can make it out clearly now: the heavy scrape of footsteps, as
harsh as steel on marble; behind these, what he assumes at first is
the suck and hiss of a factory steam engine, then realizes is actually the sound of huge, stentorian breathing. The man coming up
the stairs, he knows, is gargantuan, grotesquely fat; he fills the
stairwell plug-tight, like a moving wall of flesh. Getting past him
is impossible, the corridor is sealed. Resistance is inconceivable; if
my father remains where he is, he'll be crushed.

Turning, my father starts back up the stairs he just descended.
He begins to run. Whenever he stops to catch his breath, he can
hear the metronome tread, the fat man's breathing. He rushes on,
confident of his speed. The man is slow, after all, barely moving.
He'll simply outrun him, or keep ahead forever. The stairs unwind
like a ribbon in the wind, rising into the dark. It's then that he re-
members there is no exit; the stairwell ends in solid stone. Having
entered the dream already descending the stairs, he can only return
to where he began. Instantly sick with terror, my father turns toward
the unseen thing heaving itself up the stairs behind him, toward the
enormous bellows of the lungs, already filling the corridor with their
sound, and his own scream wrenches him awake. The year is 1932.

II

Seven years later, on March 18, 1939, my father, not yet sixteen,
stood with his friend Cyril Brana, peering excitedly through the
heavy blue curtains of his friend's second-floor apartment onto

Veveří Street, in Brno, Czechoslovakia. It had rained the night before. The dripping cables of the trolley cars, catching the light, looped thin and delicate across the city's drab pigment. Even though it was a weekday, my father said, there were no cars passing in the street below, no umbrellas hurrying down the cobbled walks or stepping over the puddles as if they were fissures into the earth, nor crowding the midstreet islands to the clanging of the trolley bell, their number suddenly doubled like inkblots on an opened paper.

Three days earlier, in an official radio message that must have seemed as unbelievable to those listening to it as the formal announcement of their own deaths, Czechoslovakia had ceased to exist. The message was delivered, as all subsequent communications would be delivered, in the declarative, staccato tones of an authority accustomed to ruling by decree, to establishing fact by fiat: Bohemia and Moravia were now the Protektorat Böhmen und Mähren, under the control of the Reichsprotektor; Slovakia, henceforth, would be an "independent" state under the German-backed Catholic clergyman Jozef Tiso.

Although the exact route the Führer's motorcade was to take through Brno had not been divulged, it was easy enough to figure out by the placement of the soldiers. Already that morning, in the drizzling half-light of dawn, long lines of dark forms could be seen along certain streets and avenues, slowly coalescing into human shapes.

The motorcade was to pass through Brno around eleven that morning. By eight, a deep, unnatural silence had settled over the city; all public transportation had been stopped, all automobile traffic forbidden. People lingered in the hallways of their apartment buildings, saying little. Military loudspeakers echoed outside, announcing that all windows onto the street were to remain closed until two o'clock. By nine-thirty, Brno was deserted.

Tired of waiting, Cyril and my father went to the kitchen for a snack. Taking turns holding a crusty loaf tight against their stomachs, they cut thick slices that they then covered with butter and a generous sediment of sugar. Half an hour later, realizing that no one would stop them—neither Cyril's father, standing strangely still a step back from the curtains of the second window, nor his mother, sitting by the piano, soundlessly crying into a red handkerchief—they made themselves some more.

Returning to the window, the two boys looked through the crack in the curtains toward the square. In the building opposite, all the curtains were drawn. Directly in front of the bookseller's shop, a German soldier in a gray-green uniform stood beside a box of small German flags on round wooden sticks. There had been no one to distribute them to. "Don't cry," said Cyril's father at one point, without turning around, so that for a moment, my father said, he seemed to be speaking to the city before him as much as to the woman behind.

"Here they come," said Cyril. The motorcade passed quickly, my father recalled, headed north, fifteen or even twenty black limousines surrounded by twice as many motorcycles, as tight as a swarm. Hitler's personal limousine, an open car, perhaps fifth in line, rode slightly apart from the others. When my father saw him, Hitler was just sitting down, his features from that second-floor window—except for a quick glimpse of jaw and mustache—almost completely obscured under the visor of his military cap. He had been standing, though to what purpose, and for whose benefit in that dead, unmoving city, one can only guess.

III

Adolf Hitler sat down. The motorcade passed, disappearing into the curtain's edge. My father took a bite of bread. Over the next six years, nearly 50 million souls would disappear into a furnace so profound it would forever wither any attempts to reckon its magnitude, caking the brain, leaving only a still, unsounded dust for which there could be no analogies, no accounting, out of which could emerge no saving truth. All that remained were apparent facts, recorded dates, accounts of events and motivations so jarring, so emotionally dissonant that they seemed to refer to some other world, a realm from which both humanity and sense had been seamlessly removed.

During the last days of the Third Reich, for example, as the concussions of Russian heavy artillery jingled the crystal in the cabinets of the Reichschancellery in Berlin, Propaganda Minister Goebbels would while away the long after-dinner hours reading to Hitler from Thomas Carlyle's history of Frederick the Great. Imagine the scene: Hitler, perhaps, at one end of a plum-colored damask sofa, his head tilted to his right hand, absentmindedly running his middle finger along the center of his brow; Goebbels in a comfortable chair opposite, one leg draped over the other, a fire companionably puffing and spitting . . .

And there, in one of the well-furnished rooms of the armor-plated, concrete-reinforced bunker beneath the Chancellery (only six years after passing through the line of sight of a fifteen-year-old boy standing behind a thick blue curtain), Adolf Hitler wept, touched by Carlyle's apostrophe to the long-dead king in the moment of his greatest trial: "Brave King! Wait yet a little while, and the days of your suffering will be over. Already the sun of your good fortune stands behind the clouds and soon will rise upon you."

Sixty feet over their heads, the nine-hundred-room Chancellery, with its polished marble halls and hundred-pound chandeliers, was methodically being pounded into dust and rubble: stacks and columns of books taken from the Chancellery libraries blocked the tall windows looking out onto the wrecked Wilhelmstrasse, the short, ugly barrels of machine guns poking between the spines; bulky crates of crosses and oak leaves barricaded the main entrance. A month earlier, Anglo-American armies had crossed the Rhine.

None of this mattered, apparently. Sensing a promise, an omen of redemption in Carlyle's description of Frederick's deliverance, Hitler and Goebbels sent a guard to retrieve the Reich's official horoscopes. And there it was: proof that, just as Prussia had been saved in the darkest hours of the Seven Years' War by the miraculous death of the czarina, so the Third Reich would survive her harshest trials. History would save her. "Even in this very year, a change of fortune shall come," Goebbels proclaimed in an eleventh-hour message to the retreating troops. "The Führer knows the exact hour of its arrival. Destiny has sent us this man so that we . . . [can] testify to the miracle . . ."

A few days later, Goebbels had his miracle, his czarina. Returning to Berlin late on the night of April 12, the capital around him rising in flames, he was approached by a secretary with urgent news: Franklin Roosevelt was dead. Phoning the news to Hitler in the bunker beneath the burning Chancellery, Goebbels was ecstatic. Here, blazingly revealed at last, was the power of Historical Necessity and Justice. The news, he felt, would revive the spirit of hope in the German people. His feelings seem to have been shared by most of the German Supreme Command. "This," wrote Finance Minister Schwerin von Krosigk in his diary, "was the Angel of History! We felt its wings flutter through the room."

Less than two weeks later, in the cramped air-raid shelter of the Ministry of the People's Enlightenment and Propaganda, Goebbels's six children lay dead, their lips, eyes, arms, and legs turned blue from the potassium cyanide pills given to them by their father. Goebbels's wife, Magda, who had apparently dressed the children for the occasion, was also dead, shot by her husband, who then poured gasoline on her and set fire to her skirt. Goebbels himself, after killing his family, poured gasoline on his clothes, set fire to a trouser leg, then turned the gun to his temple. Across the Wilhelmplatz, German gunners lay buried beneath the crumbled barricades of books, the high-ceilinged rooms behind

them wavering in the heat of raging fires. In a small room in the
bunker below, having rejected poison after watching the agonized
deaths of the Chancellery dogs, Adolf Hitler sat down on a deep-
cushioned brocade sofa next to the body of his bride, Eva Braun,
put a gun in his mouth, and pulled the trigger. Blood flowed down
and coagulated on the brocade. The Angel of History fluttered its
wings.

IV

Thirty-four years later, on one of those drizzling October afternoons in New York City when dusk sets in at noon, they fluttered
again. An undergraduate at Columbia College at the time, I'd found
myself more than usually broke, and, reaching the limits of my in-
ventiveness on the hot plate, I decided to find a job. In a small office off the claustrophobic circular hallway in the basement of Low
Library, I answered an ad for something called Student Help for the
Elderly. After filling out a long questionnaire, I was given the name
of one Beatrix Turner, an address on 69th Street off Broadway, and
told when to appear. The job paid three-fifty an hour.

I didn't want it. Between classes and sleeping with a young
woman I'd met at Barnard that fall (or rather not sleeping, never
sleeping), I felt exhausted, perpetually late to everything, always
sprinting bleary-eyed up Claremont Avenue or leaping puddles
on the way to some overheated classroom where a professor whose
name I couldn't remember would already be discussing whatever
author—Hobbes or Locke, Nietzsche or Kant—I'd failed to finish reading the night before. When I added to this the hundred-
block walk down Broadway and back (I begrudged the bus fare),
the fact that it always seemed to be raining on the days I had to
go, and, finally, that I'd be skipping two classes a week (I'd had
to lie on my application to get the job), it seemed like a bad deal.
I took the job anyway.

I don't remember Beatrix Turner very well, just a small, well-kept woman in a bone-white dress given to straight talk and strong opinions. I remember that her apartment, small even by dormitory standards, was very cluttered, very still. Everything sounded louder there: the door down the hall, the spoon in the cup, the tiny steps of the minute hand drawing its harvest of days on the mantle. She showed me how to make tea for her with whole cinnamon, cloves, and ginger, and for years afterward, though I'd never particularly enjoyed being there (she was cranky and irritable; I, no doubt, sullen and impatient), these smells were my mildly unpleasant madeleines, dragging me, willy-nilly, back to that apartment on 69th Street, my unmourned Combray by the Hudson.

And so, on the misty, gray afternoon of October 2, I started down Broadway to Beatrix Turner's apartment, moving quickly through the crowd, dodging trucks on 110th Street, checking out the nickel-and-dime bodegas where I bought the odds and ends I needed for my dormitory room. To compensate for my jeans and sneakers, I'd thrown on my one good jacket. Ten blocks north of Sherman Square, with the rain beginning to come down in earnest and umbrellas opening all around me like strange black blooms, I took it off, folded it under my arm, and sprinted for 69th Street.

I found Beatrix Turner in a reflective mood that afternoon. The tea, as I recall, had already been made; the chores, she said, could wait. Toweling off as best I could, I wiped my streaming glasses on a napkin and, balancing my cup and saucer awkwardly on my lap, sat down in the chair she indicated. I looked around the apartment. I'd never noticed the mementos before—the framed letters, the ribbons, the statuary. There was something oddly moving about that crowded menagerie. Everywhere I looked the small faces of men and women (many in British or American World War II uniforms, some with their arms around each other, all very young) smiled down out of the photographs that lined the book-shelves and the walls of that apartment, a tiny eternal audience come to witness the final act of Beatrix Turner's long performance. A pretty young woman in an Air Force cap sat on the hood of a jeep. A rough-looking young man in a black sweater (his teeth closed tight and his brow furrowed as though he were squinting into the sun) looked out from what I took to be the loops and bars of his own overbold signature, written across the sky.

The spiced tea tasted good that afternoon. Every now and again the radiator, as though harboring some furious apartment gnome, would begin to clang and ping and whine. Past the safety grates and the slowly rusting fire escape, I could see the rain. The blinds in the windows across the air shaft were shut. Inexplicably mellow that afternoon (or perhaps just resigned to my ignorance), Beatrix Turner began to talk. Her voice, ordinarily strong, decidedly un-gentle, now softened. It seemed to me then, though the details are lost, that she'd been nearly everywhere, done almost everything—drank ouzo with Hemingway, danced with Dos Passos. Some of her accounts were more obscure, and for long stretches I listened to stories of people I'd never heard of, places that held no mean-ing for me, selfishly grateful that I didn't have to scrub an already spotless sink or look, yet again, for the reading glasses that she had just had a second before; grateful too, I'll admit now, for the fact that I was closing in on ten dollars and fifty cents without yet having done a stitch of work.

But then I started to listen. Beatrix Turner, I realized, had been a war correspondent through much of 1944 and 1945. She'd been with the American First Army when it met the Russians at Torgau on the Elbe River. And on May 3 or 4, traveling on foot, she'd entered Berlin.

The city had fallen the day before. Where the crumbling out-lines of foundations and rooms showed through the piled rubble, they seemed, as though escaping their own reality, to hark backward or forward to the very ancient or the purely ephemeral, to some Neolithic civilization, recently unearthed, or to a child's sand castle, broken by the tide. On the bullet-chipped walls and columns of the Reichstag, now a blackened shell, Russian names, scrawled by the living, memorialized those who had died for victory. Somehow making her way to the Chancellery through that heaped, smoldering city—whether alone or accompanied I don't remember—Beatrix Turner arrived to discover that Russian engineers had already burned the hinges off the heavy steel doors facing the smoking garden.

She leaned forward. "You know, of course, that Adolf Hitler shot himself in his bunker beneath the Chancellery."

I began to say something, but she waved it away.

"Oh, that's all bosh about Paraguay and Argentina," she said. "He shot himself. Eva Braun took arsenic."

I didn't say anything.

Beatrix Turner took a sip of tea. "I was one of the first ones down," she said.

I don't remember if Beatrix Turner told me how she talked her way past the guards that day, nor can I be certain whether the image I have of her descending those endless, pitch-black stairs by candlelight or flashlight is based on the description she gave me or the ones I've read since then. In the entry I wrote in my journal later that night, there's no mention of the cold, dank smell of extinguished fires, of the charred picture frames, like overdrawn metaphors, still hanging from the walls, of the black water, ankle deep, that covered the carpets.

But one memory remains as clear as on the night I wrote it down. Sensing my skepticism, perhaps, Beatrix Turner put down her cup and saucer and went to a closet near the front door. "I have something to show you," she said. "A little souvenir." I stood up, thinking to help her, but she was already carrying an ordinary cardboard carton. Placing it on the table, she opened it, removed another, smaller carton, and from this a carefully folded wad of tissue. Unwrapping this bundle, she revealed a fragile piece of cloth with a strange, almost Egyptian-looking pattern, marred by an ugly dark stain.

I looked at the thing, uncomprehending.

"I cut this piece out of the sofa in the bunker," Beatrix Turner said. She pointed. "That's Adolf Hitler's blood."

Before I could say anything, she was leafing through an old issue of *Life* she'd brought out of the closet with her, and suddenly there it was: a photograph of correspondents, one holding a candle, inspecting the richly patterned brocade sofa on which Adolf Hitler and Eva Braun had committed suicide. In the photograph, one could see the pattern of the sofa clearly, a repeating motif of male figures dressed in traditional folk garb standing next to huge, orchidlike blooms, or fanciful palms, or exploding fireworks. Each figure held a sort of leash that dipped in a lazy *U* to the neck of a prancing stag.

On the right armrest, a dark, vaguely phallic bloodstain had soaked the brocade, obliterating half a leash and half a stag. I looked at the piece of cloth I now held in my hand. The stag was nearly gone; only its hooves and hindquarters remained. The pattern matched.

I left the apartment soon afterward. Waiting for the elevator, I noticed a door at the far end of the hall. I pushed it open. Four flights down a badly lit stairwell brought me to a locked door. Looking around, I saw another, smaller door. Forcing it open, I saw that it led out onto a fire escape. A fixed steel ladder dropped twenty feet to the alley below. I climbed out, soiling my jacket against the rusting frame. Even today I can remember the good strong sting of the rain against my face. At the bottom of the unlit, cluttered alley, rising like a canyon to the sky, I pushed open the heavy iron gate to 69th Street and started to run.

Coda

Pleasure and pain are immediate; knowledge, retrospective. A steel ball, suspended on a string, smacks into its brothers and nothing happens: no shock of recognition, no sudden epiphany. We go about our business, buttering the toast, choosing gray socks over brown. But here's the thing: just because we haven't understood something doesn't mean we haven't been shaped by it. Although I couldn't understand what I'd seen in Beatrix Turner's apartment that autumn afternoon in 1979, although I ran the way a child will run, stopping up its ears, from something dark and grotesque, something far beyond its years, the deed had been done. That cloth, in its own pathetic way, dealt a featuring blow to my life.

What I reacted to—instinctively, I suppose—was the terrible smallness of the thing, the almost vertiginous compaction of the symbol. Behind that ridiculous cloth with its vaguely shit-brown stain, I could sense the nations of the dead pushing and jostling for space, for room, for a voice; it was as though all the sounds of the world had been drawn into the plink of a single drop falling from the lip of a loosened drain. One could resist the implicit lesson, recognize the obscenity of linking that worthless piece of fabric to the murder of millions, even note the small irony of its being preserved, like some unholy relic, from the disintegration it implied, and yet still be moved by an inescapable thought, a thought both unjust and unavoidable: that it should come to this, O God asleep in heaven, a tattered piece of cloth in an apartment on 69th Street.

But of course, it didn't. History resists an ending as surely as nature abhors a vacuum; the narrative of our days is a run-on sentence, every full stop a comma in embryo. But more: like thought, like water, history is fluid, unpredictable, dangerous. It leaps and surges and doubles back, cuts unpredictable channels, surfaces suddenly in places no one would expect. How else can one explain

the dream that foreshadows the event? Or fear immaculately con-
ceived? Or a will to resistance that reemerges, inexplicably, continents and generations from where it fell?

And so, perhaps, it comes down to this: that the irresistible
march of events through time—the cup raised, the drink taken,
the sudden knock on the door—is the only truth we have and
yet, and I don't mean to be clever here, the greatest lie we tell.
The empire of facts is irrefutable; death *will* have its dominion.
Recognizing the limits of chronology, resisting its unforgiving
dictates, is our duty and our right. There is no contradiction.

Arrow and Wound

2003

Five years before his death in 1986, Jaroslav Seifert, the unofficial poet laureate of Prague (and official Nobel laureate of Stockholm), published *Všecky krásy světa (All the Beauties of the Earth)*, a book that was neither autobiography nor history nor fiction, precisely, but all of these and more: a gallery of small, precise portraits, each characteristically anchored in the mind's eye by a single, telling anecdote: a peddler's cart, picturesque with eight decades' worth of well-turned stories and three o'clock in the morning, second-bottle speculations summoning a past both personal and, inevitably, cultural. In short, a celebration and a leave-taking: tender, spendthrift, large. A visitor to Tolstoy's Yasnaya Polyana recalled seeing the count, then in his last years, scoop a double handful of violets from the wet earth, breathe in their aroma with a kind of ecstasy, then let them fall carelessly at his feet. That gesture, captured on paper, is Seifert's book.

But this is not about *Všecky krásy světa*, exactly, nor is it about Tolstoy. It is about a curious little section near the book's center, in which Seifert—no decadent after all, no Baudelaire—admits to having once been jealous of another writer's near-death experience. That other writer was Fyodor Mikhailovich Dostoevsky.

The incident at Semenovsky Square that winter morning of

December 22, 1849, when Dostoevsky and his fellow subversives
were led before the firing squad in a mock execution, then pardoned at the last moment in order to impress upon them the full
magnitude of the czar's mercy, is well known; like Byron's inces-
tuous relationship with his half sister, say, or Wilde's self-aided
lynching, it has passed out of literary biography and joined that
select company of events the generally literate misremember with
confidence. Still, the narrative of those hours, progressing like a
medieval passion play from suffering to near-death to something
like resurrection, remains compelling. Reconstituted in the willing imagination, it can stab us, suddenly, unexpectedly, with the
quickening thought of our own extinction—a nectar not to be indulged in too often, lest it become a self-indulgence, an obscenity.

Imagine it, then. The sounds of voices and carriages in the
prison courtyard that morning. The church bells, uncharacteris-
tically diminished by the sound of cell doors opening down the
corridor—the sudden, irrepressible, dizzying thought of freedom.
You are given your clothes—the ones you were arrested in eight
months ago—and told to remember to put on your socks, for the
morning is cold. You must hurry. No one answers your questions.

Dawn. You are led into the snowy yard. A line of carriages
stands waiting, flanked by mounted police. Your comrades are
there; you see Speshnev, peering out of a shaggy mat of tangled
hair and matted beard, and then you are in the carriage. The windows are covered with frost. Perhaps you scratch at the pane with
a fingernail. Perhaps the guard sitting next to you lets you. You
want to see the world. God in heaven, you say to yourself, it's over.
A day, a week, a month, whatever it takes for the process to run its
course, and it will be over. You'll see your brother again. You'll be
able to release the stories burgeoning in your mind, threatening
to burst your skull. You'll be free.

The line of carriages comes to a stop. Semenovsky Square lies
under a foot of snow. The sun appears and disappears behind the

mist. Soldiers stand around the perimeter of the square. A small crowd has gathered on the far end. You wait around in the snow, talking excitedly with your old comrades. No one knows what is happening. A four-sided wooden scaffolding, draped in black crepe, stands in the center of the square. Probably you will be sentenced to some time of penal servitude, lectured on your presumption and ingratitude. There are worse things.

It is then, maybe, that you first notice the row of head-high stakes, like great, fat nails holding down the field of snow.

Or do you? In the sudden shock of knowing (which instantly reshapes the minutes remaining into a strange, circumscribed eternity, an ocean disappearing down a drain), can a person think at all, much less in metaphor? What really happens in those final few moments? Does the world, under the pressure of extinction, blossom into tropes as never before, madly, ferociously, birthing stakes like Christic nails, or crosses symbolically shorn of the horizontal, or huge, ironic exclamation points? Does it, instead, taper down to some small perfection—the godhead glimpsed in a drop of sweat, freezing to a pearl? Or does the world simply bend its head and grow mute, and you with it? And if it does, isn't it possible that, should you be miraculously delivered out of that silence by the czar's pardon, you would emerge with a voice that could speak the truths of this world with a clarity unavailable to others? That you would be repaid for your suffering—as is sometimes the case, after all—in the coin of wisdom?

It would be nice to think so. Which brings us back to Seifert, who did. "Though fully aware of the impossibility of drawing a comparison between us," he writes, self-effacingly, "I envied Dostoevsky . . . that singular experience: to be sentenced to death, to know the moment when you must, of necessity, say good-bye to life, accept that unappeasable fact, and then taste again the certainty and sweetness of life, and save yourself." The notion compelled him, fascinated him. "To experience those few, horrifying minutes when time is quickly dragging you to your erasure," he continues, "and then to look again upon the broad expanse of time that stretches out before you like a gorgeous landscape. What a drama it must be, which plays itself out in a man during those few instants! What does an experience like that mean, for anyone, but particularly for a writer, who has the ability to articulate it?"*

Seifert had been able to answer that question for himself. Saturday, May 5, 1945, found him, then forty-four years old, in the Lidové building on Hybernská Street in Prague, laboring, along with a small crew of fellow journalists, to bring out the next edition of the newly decriminalized newspaper *Rudé právo*. Outside their windows, the stylus of history had begun to move, inscribing another bloody paragraph. After six years of occupation, the fingers of the Reich had begun suddenly to loosen. In a frenzy of rage and joy, Czechs of all ages began demolishing German businesses, lighting fires, erecting barricades. The Prague uprising had begun.

It would take its measure of lives before it was done. As Seifert and his companions soon learned, the Germans had taken a stand in the Anglobank building just down the way. The concussion of cannon and the staccato pattering of small-arms fire filled the street, windows shattered; the Masaryk train station was in flames. Seeking safety from the cross fire, the entire staff, along with a group of citizens who had taken shelter with them, moved down to the basement, then lower still, into the paper-storage rooms, and continued writing. Days passed. They barely ate. Somehow, the presses continued to roll.

And then, as Seifert tells it, things turned. Quickly. The Germans retook the train station. From there, they captured the building on the corner of Hybernská and Havlíčková streets and entered the system of passageways connecting the buildings' cellars. And

---

* All translations by the author.

suddenly Seifert and his comrades were being marched to the
train station, where, they were informed, they would be executed.
Just like that. In the station, their shoes sticky with blood, they
stood by a heap of dead Czechs while the Germans worked to
dispatch a train filled with tier upon tier of their own wounded.
They waited. A young boy, found with an antique bayonet under
his coat, was shot in the back of the neck.

When the train didn't leave, they were led back out, two by
two. Buildings were burning. The heat was immense. They were
lined up against a wall, presently, and told they would be shot in
the courtyard behind them as soon as it was empty of German
families preparing to flee. And again they waited.

So what did Seifert do, those ostensibly last few minutes of
his life? What did he think? This was it, after all—the experience he had envied Dostoevsky. This was consciousness in the
crucible, distilled to its essence. Did the heat of those minutes
crystallize his understanding into some new, unbreakable alloy?
Reorder his life?

Apparently not. Standing against the wall next to his friend
Píša, waiting to be shot, Seifert discovered a piece of bread and
some cheese, no longer quite fresh, in his pocket. The two ate it
hungrily. For a few moments, he tells us, he thought about his
family. He knew they were relatively safe. The thought that he
might never see them again did not occur to him. He looked at
the buildings across the street. All the windows were closed. Now
and then a corner of a curtain lifted slightly and a face appeared.
Then, far off, he spotted the public toilet by the Karlín viaduct and
suddenly recalled how, when he was a boy, someone had drawn a
wonderfully obscene picture of a woman on one of its walls, and
how he and his friends would walk kilometers just to look at it.
How it had aroused and disturbed them. Then he looked again at
the buildings across the street. Smoke rose languidly out of the
chimneys. He found himself wondering what the people inside,

who didn't have to stand with their backs against a wall, were
making for lunch.

Then, after twenty minutes or half an hour had passed, he and
the others were informed that they could go.

And that was that, claims Seifert. The condemned scattered
in all directions. And when, soon afterward, the city's radios an-
nounced that Nazi Germany had officially capitulated and that
the war in Europe was effectively over, they forgot all about what
had just passed. Seifert himself never thought of it. Decades later,
finding himself in that same district of the city, he actually passed
by the very wall he had stood against that fateful day, and never
even realized it until after he'd arrived home and was sitting down
to dinner.

So much for Semenovsky Square. So much for the romance of
almost dying. Pushed to the wall, given ample time to consider his
situation, to breathe, to weep, Seifert had eaten lunch. No epiphany. No prophetic voice, rising out of the silence. Nothing.

Compare and contrast. Standing in the snow in Semenovsky
Square, Dostoevsky experienced a kind of "mystic terror," a strange
and fearful exaltation. "Nous serons avec le Christ" ("We shall
be with Christ"), he supposedly whispered to Speshnev, quoting
Victor Hugo's *Le dernier jour d'un condamné*. Seifert just looked
at the ugly buildings across the street. From the moment the
roll of the drums signaled to him that his life would be spared,
Dostoevsky's life had shifted course, surging, like a river around
an insurmountable obstacle, toward the kind of tortured religios-
ity we now associate with his greatest work. Seifert? Seifert was
untouched. Life went on. Thirty-five years later, writing about the
hour he had expected to be his last, he recalled (not without some
small, remembered pleasure) a picture of a spread-eagled woman
drawn with a piece of coal on the side of a public toilet.

Whose version do we believe? I suspect that the romantics

among us (as well as the more conventionally and narrowly devout) side with Dostoevsky. And perhaps the rest of us do as well. How could a person not be touched, altered, by such an experience? We don't want to be like an old horse led to the slaughter. We want awareness, insight. We want to believe that our consciousness, like putty, will take the imprint of great events. Suffer, and ye shall be rewarded with, if nothing else, the memory of your suffering. No, when it comes to the art of almost dying, Dostoevsky is our man.

Literature backs us up. "They are not to lose it," intones Faulkner, referring to the witnesses of Joe Christmas's murder in *Light in August*, "in whatever peaceful valleys, beside whatever placid and reassuring streams of old age, in the mirroring faces of whatever children they will contemplate old disasters and newer hopes." Yes, indeed, we say. Just so. And although we recognize the fact that Faulkner's narrator, unlike Dostoevsky, contemplates his own extinction only by proxy, as it were, he still flatters our sense of the gravity of the thing, our notion of what it ought to be like. Death is a big deal, after all. If it frightens us, it ought to be large.

What of Seifert, then? Do we write off his amnesia as denial, debunk him with a pinch of Freud? Do we see his parable of the bread and the public toilet for what it is: a re-presentation of events, an attempt to impose a shape, nearly thirty-six years afterward, on a harrowing, unmanageable experience—in sum, a fiction? Do we classify it, perhaps, as an absurdist and in many ways classically Czech response to trauma? Do we pat the author on the head and leave him to carve his figures in the tranquillity of old age?

I think not. To do so, it seems to me, would be to assume that consciousness can be teased apart from its retelling, which it cannot. To see Dostoevsky's experience as essentially truthful, and Seifert's as some form of artifice, is to limit the dominion of fiction, which, from the moment we wake to the power of language, rules our lives with czarist authority and reach. It is also to forget a more intriguing and complicated truth: that we in some measure shape the events that befall us just as surely as we are shaped by them.

There is no point in being coy; I am indulging in these kinds of end-time speculations because I, too, was once given the "singular experience" of believing that I had arrived at the terminus of my life, of seeing myself dragged to the brink of my own erasure, only to be pardoned at the last minute by some combination of arrangement and accident. Like Seifert and Dostoevsky (in this way if in no other), I was given the opportunity to know my last minutes on earth. I didn't care for it.

My case was different, of course. Apolitical, ahistorical—set, above all, in the New World wilderness rather than in a European square—it lacked both the cruelty of Dostoevsky's mock execution and the context of routine and unimaginable suffering that backlights Seifert's ordeal. My experience, in short, was smaller. No one's life was at stake besides my own and that of the woman who was to become my wife. I suppose that in the spirit of charity I might add the life of the man who seemed to have decided to take our lives along with his own. That makes three. That morning, it seemed enough.

Quickly, then. The year was 1985. My wife and I (to see her as anything but my wife now seems like an affectation) had just crossed the spine of the Sierras. We were in our late twenties. That July morning we were hitchhiking back to the San Joaquin Valley. I knew the area, a harsh and perpendicular landscape of considerable beauty, from some years earlier, when I had worked with a crew doing trail maintenance in the backcountry. I knew, therefore, that there were two roads to the western side of the Sierra Nevada: a highway looping around the foot of the range, and a rarely taken shortcut through the town of Lake Isabella.

We started out at first light, eager to avoid as much of the desert heat as possible, joking in the coolness. Our first three rides were uneventful. We saw the fourth from far off, a large white car, approaching the highway at an oblique angle on a ruler-straight road, raising a wall of dust. It was coming very quickly. Perhaps a quarter mile behind us, the car came to a stop, then gunned out onto the highway. It never crossed my mind that it would stop for us. I would have bet everything I had against it.

I remember him getting out of his car—thick, steak-fed body, sun-red face, not unkind—and asking us if we wanted to put our things in his trunk. "Give you kids some room," he said. He called us kids. I remember him arranging and rearranging our battered packs, closing the trunk carefully to avoid damaging something. I remember the blue jacket on the passenger seat with its Kern County Fire Department insignia; he drove casually, a thick right arm around the seat next to him as though around an invisible companion. We made small talk—hitchhiking etiquette. He asked where we were headed. We told him. He was going to Bakersfield, too, he said. We were in luck. We asked if he lived there. No, he lived in the Owens Valley. My wife asked politely what took him to Bakersfield. He laughed. "Well, it's like this," he said. "My mother had a massive heart attack at 10:15 this morning. They're trying to keep her alive until I get there."

Somewhere inside, an alarm went off. A small herd of questions, like panicked horses, stampeded across the landscape. Why would a man racing to his mother's deathbed stop to pick up two hitchhikers? Why would he take five minutes to arrange their packs in his trunk? Why would he be so calm, so level, so apparently undisturbed?

And yet, on the surface, everything seemed fine. He was driving well enough—a bit casually, perhaps, a bit faster than necessary, but well within the normal range. When we expressed our condolences, he thanked us politely. The minutes passed. No further warnings came. For a few moments, I considered asking him to let us out in the town of Lake Isabella on some pretext, but, stymied by my inability to think of a good excuse as well as, more damnably, by my own sense of politeness (the man was doing us a favor, after all), I said nothing.

In retrospect, my own inertia staggers me. I knew what lay ahead: a twenty-mile stretch of unimproved canyon road running, at times, a full 150 feet above the Kern River. A road so narrow that the few cars that did take it would invariably stop at every turn and honk to make sure no one was approaching from the other direction. A road without walls or guardrails of any kind. I had taken it twice, years before, to save the four hours, and driven it, each time, at barely over walking speed.

He stopped at the cattle guard where the canyon road began and turned half around over his right shoulder. He was smiling, but he looked as though he were about to cry. "Don't forget those seat belts, kids," he said, like a television announcer on the verge of a nervous breakdown. That same instant he stomped on the gas.

Let me dispense with the rational right off: This was not, for example, a superb if reckless driver testing his skill, or some variety of local daredevil, intimately familiar with the landscape, out to terrify the college kids. This was something entirely different. This was a man in such pain that he no longer cared to live; a man calmly holding a revolver to his temple and, with four chambers empty, two to go, pulling the trigger. This was a man making a bet with God—or lunging at him. It's quite possible that he himself had no idea why he had picked us up. In some essential way, we were beside the point.

What followed was madness. We skidded blindly into turn after turn, fishtailed down the straights. Again and again we sideswiped the wall with a sickening screech of metal and bounced toward the edge. Once, twice, three times, I felt the right rear wheel begin to drop, felt the car begin to lighten, sickeningly, sensed the pull of the canyon air below us.

So what did I think of, those thirty minutes or so? Nothing very original, I'm afraid. I remember realizing, with a mixture of rage and disbelief, that this was it. That my life, our life, was somehow, impossibly, over. I remember my mind racing, searching for options. Hit the crazy bastard? Unthinkable. There was no margin. We were over the margin already. Try to say something, calm him somehow? Impossible. He was elsewhere now. And I knew, as surely as I've ever known anything, that if I said even one word, he would turn around to look at me and simply turn the wheel into the empty air.

I'll confess that I did not believe we would live. I knew the road we were on. We had nearly gone over a half dozen times already, and there were sixteen or seventeen miles of curves still ahead. My wife, a genuinely brave woman, had buried her face in my shirt.

But here's the thing: although I knew we weren't going to make it, my mind, divided against itself, stupidly refused to accept that fact. And so, never a religious man, I did the only thing I could: I willed that car to stay on the road. Irrational? Absurd? Of course. And yet that is what I did. As though it were possible. As though, like those sad individuals forever trying to bend spoons with their minds, I could simply force the physical world's attention. As though reality were that malleable. And the mind that crude a weapon. I willed that car not to go over, to hold. I fought for every inch. Rigid with fear, I drove those twenty miles like a ghost inside his body, wrestling for the wheel, turning the skid, forcing us, again and again, back to the wall.

But enough of that. We lived. When we emerged from the canyon, he slowed, and when I asked him, as soon as I was able to speak, to please let us out, he pulled over on the shoulder. I could barely get out of the car. I was soaked in sweat, clenched tight as a fist. He pulled away, leaving us standing by our packs in the desert heat.

For a minute, as though embarrassed by something, we didn't speak. Then we slipped on our packs and walked across the road to a store of some kind, where we treated ourselves to a cold soda. It was over.

It's not the experience that interests me here. The event itself, after all, was almost banal: two kids catch the proverbial bad ride, and don't die. So what? What interests me is the aftermath, the effect.

For almost twenty years, you see, I didn't know there was an effect. We went on. We finished our soda, married, had children. Along the way, I began to write. We didn't forget, à la Seifert, what had happened to us—far from it. We told the tale again and again. For twenty years we regaled new friends with it, tricked it up like a pet poodle and made it dance about, bored each other silly with it. In time, it came to have nothing to do with us. Although all the essential details were still there (altered just enough to spare ourselves the pain of an identical retelling), it had became a pose, a self-dramatizing tic, an amusing story recounted over dinner ("And that's when he turned to me—by the way, what do you think of this wine?—and said . . .").

What I didn't realize was that the thing itself had gone underground. And although it surfaced periodically, sometimes in ways almost laughably obvious, I remained oblivious to it. In a recurrent nightmare that visited me perhaps once a year—to take just one, particularly humiliating, example—I would be behind the wheel of a car, my wife beside me, when it plunged over the side of some impossible height: wind whistling against the steel, and a realization that there was nothing to be done, no way to live. And yet, through all those years, I swear I did not make the connection. I assumed, for some reason, that I had always had this particular dream. My blindness, at times, was comical. When the melodramatic ending of *Thelma & Louise* made me almost physically ill, I wrote it off as a token neurosis—my little burden—and thought nothing more of it.

The lid did not come off the pot for seventeen years—until the day I found myself, so to speak, walking past the wall where I had expected to die. Unlike Seifert, however, I knew precisely where I was and what I was there for. Turning up the road from Lake Isabella, my wife beside me and our children in the back seat, I stopped at the cattle guard, then drove the road again. Slowly. By the time we emerged from the shadow of the canyon walls, I understood (no blare of trumpets here, no flash of revelation) the genesis of all those years of dreams, and knew, as well, that I was shut of them forever.

Time makes liars of us all. The moment passes; our words alone are left us. An obvious truth. That our character can prefigure an event as well as be shaped by one, that reality and consciousness are mutually dependent, is, perhaps, less obvious. Did the twenty-eight-year-old Dostoevsky really quote Hugo while waiting to be tied to a stake and shot, as his comrade F. N. Lvov remembered a decade later? Did Jaroslav Seifert really remember a picture on a public toilet, then wonder idly what the people across the way were making for lunch? Should we see the letter Dostoevsky wrote to his brother immediately after the ordeal as an accurate representation of his thoughts those last few minutes in Semenovsky Square, or read the famous mock-execution scene in *The Idiot*, written some twenty years later, as the truest depiction of what he endured that December morning? Should you, finally, believe my retelling of the ride we caught that summer day in 1985, or accept my recollections of what went through my mind those few minutes? Should I?

Yes and no. Every retelling is inevitably a distortion, but that does not mean it is without value. We can't help but tell the truth. Although we will never know what Dostoevsky experienced that

December morning in Semenovsky Square, we can, from his re-telling, with its particular fingerprint of stresses and omissions, learn a great deal about him. Although we will never know what Jaroslav Seifert really thought or felt standing against that wall (although he himself may no longer know—indeed, may never have known), we can see, with perfect clarity, what he wants us to believe he thought or felt. Nothing reveals us as clearly as our attempt to shape the past. Retrospection is, by definition, reflexive.

What our inadvertent self-portrait reveals, if we study it closely enough, is that our consciousness, rather than being shaped by a particular event, predated it. That we were, in a sense, anticipating it. That, to recall Kafka's haunting insight, "the arrows fit exactly in the wounds" for which they were intended. Dostoevsky experienced what he did in Semenovsky Square because he was Dostoevsky. Because he already carried inside him, like a patient wound, the "cursed questions" he would seek to answer the rest of his life. Seifert, the poet of the quotidian and the small, thought about the things he did because he was Jaroslav Seifert, the man who, thirty-five years later, would write a book called *All the Beauties of the Earth*. Because, like Tolstoy at Yasnaya Polyana, he gathered the things of this life, and let them fall at his feet. The experience, in other words, was already prepared for him by the time he got there. As it is, to some extent, for all of us.

As for me, I had been driving that canyon road all my life. In all my work, in all my deepest imaginings, tragedy had always been invited, played with, then sent on its way. How appropriate, then, how predictable, that it would do the same for me.

There's the event, waiting for us. And we fit it as perfectly as the arrow fits its wound.

Listening for Silence

1999

Music, Claude Debussy once famously remarked, is the stuff between the notes, an observation that resonates, pardon the pun, from the flawless spacing of a Billie Holiday tune to the deletions—whether generous or cruel—in our daily lives. Essentially neuter, neither balm nor curse, silence, like light or love, requires a medium to give it meaning, takes on the color of its host, adapts easily to our fears and needs. Quite apart from whether we seek or shun it, silence orchestrates the music of our days.

I'm well aware, of course, that one man's music is another man's noise, that the primary differences between a cork-lined room and solitary confinement are the lock on the door and the sensibility of the inmate. I wish not to define silence but to inquire about its absence, and I ask the question not to restate the obvious—that silence, in its way, is fundamental to life, the emotional equivalent of carbon—but because everywhere I turn I see a culture willing to deny that essential truth. In my idle moments I picture a god from my son's book of myths (with an Olympian straw and sucked-in cheeks) drawing the silence out of the land, and if the conceit is fanciful, the effect, sadly, is not: as silence disappears, the world draws tighter, borders collapse, the public and private bleed and intermix. Victim to the centripetal pull, the imagination crackles with the static of outside frequencies, while somewhere in the soul—listen!—a cell phone is chirping. Answer it quickly, before someone else does.

At the close of the millennium, a new Tower of Babel, monolingual despite the superficial mixture of tongues, homogeneous because almost invariably pitched in the vernacular of the marketplace, casts its shadow over the land. Ubiquitous, damn near inescapable, it is rearranging the way we live, forcing crucial adjustments in our behavior, straining our capacity for adaptation. If it continues to grow, as I believe it will, future generations may one day distinguish our age not for its discovery of Elsewhere, as E. B. White called the world beyond the television screen, but for its colonization of silence.

Ensnared in webs of sound, those of us living in the industrialized West today must pick our way through a discordant, infinite-channeled auditory landscape. Like a radio stuck on permanent scan, the culture lashes us with skittering bits and bytes, each dragging its piece of historical or emotional context: a commercial overheard in traffic, a falsely urgent weather report, a burst of canned laughter, half a refrain. The cell phone interrupts lectures, sermons, second acts, and funerals. Everywhere a new song begins before the last one ends, as though to guard us against even the potential of silence. Each place we turn, a new world—synthetic, fragmented, often as not jacked into the increasingly complex grid that makes up the global communications network—encroaches on the old world of direct experience, of authentic, unadorned events with their particular, unadorned sounds.

Although a great deal has been said about our increasingly visual age, the changes to our aural landscape have gone relatively unremarked. The image has grown so voracious that any child asked to sum up the century will instantly visualize Einstein's hair and Hitler's mustache, mushroom clouds and the moon landing, despite the fact that each of these visual moments has its aural correlative, from the blast over Hiroshima to the high-pitched staccato ravings of the Führer to Neil Armstrong's static-ridden "giant leap for mankind."

But make no mistake: sound will have its dominion. The aural universe, though subtler than the one that imprints itself on our retina, is more invasive, less easily blocked. It mocks our sanctuaries as light never can. If my neighbor decides to wash his car in front of my study window, as he does often, I can block out the uninspiring sight of his pimpled posterior by drawing the shades; to block out his stereo, I must kill noise with noise. We hear in our sleep. There is no aural equivalent for the eyelid. In our day, when the phone can ring, quite literally, anywhere on the planet, this is not necessarily good news.

I have nothing against my aural canal. I adore music (though I make it badly). I have nothing against a good party, the roar of the crowd. But I make a distinction between nourishment and gluttony: the first is a necessity, even a pleasure; the second, a symptom. Of what? In a word, fear. One of the unanticipated side effects of connectedness. Perhaps because it's never enough, or because, having immersed ourselves in the age of mediation (as Bill Gates refers to it), accustomed ourselves to its ways and means, we sense our dependency. Or because, like isolated apartment dwellers running the television for company, we sense a deeper isolation beneath the babble of voices, the poverty of our communications. So, adaptable to a fault, we embrace this brave new cacophony, attuned, like apprentice ornithologists, to the distinguishing calls of a mechanical phylum. Capable of differentiating between the cheeps and chimes of the cell phones, portable phones, baby monitors, pagers, scanners, laptops, car alarms, and so on that fill our lives, we've grown adept, at the same time, at blocking them out with sounds of our own, at forcing a privacy where none exists.

At the supermarket, a middle-aged man in a well-cut suit is

calling someone a bitch on the phone. Unable to get to the ricotta cheese, I wait, vaguely uncomfortable, feeling as though I'm eaves-dropping. At the gym, the beeps of computerized treadmills clash with the phones at the front desk, the announcements of upcom-ing discounts, the disco version of Gordon Lightfoot's "If You Could Read My Mind." A number of individuals in Walkman earphones, unaware that they've begun to sing, bellow and moan like the deaf.

"I love a wide margin to my life," Thoreau remarked, quaintly, referring to the space—the silence—requisite for contemplation, or, more quaintly, the forming of a self. A century and a half later, aural text covers the psychic page, spills over; the margin is gone. Walking to work, we pass over rumbling pipes and humming cables, beneath airplane flight corridors and satellite broadcasts, through radio and television transmissions whose sounds, reconstituted from binary code, mix and mingle, overlap and crash, and everywhere drifts the aural refuse of our age.

Thus may the stuff between the discordant notes of our lives require—and I'm not unaware of the irony here—a few words in its defense. Begin anywhere. The cottage in which I spend my summers is silent yet full of sound: the rainy hush of wind in the oaks, the scrabble of a hickory nut rolling down the roof, the slurp of the dog in the next room, interminably licking himself . . . I've never known perfect silence. I hope to avoid making its acquain-tance for some time to come, yet I court it daily.

My ambivalence toward silence is natural enough: the grave, the scythe, the frozen clock, all the piled symbols of death, re-inforce an essential truth, a primal fear: beneath the sloping hood, death is voiceless. Silence spits us out and engulfs us again, one and all, and all the noisemakers on Bourbon Street, all the clat-tering figurines in Cuernavaca can't undo the unpleasant fact that *el día,* properly understood, always ends in *la muerte,* that quiet, like a pair of giant parentheses around a dependent clause, closes off our days. Sorry.

But if it's true that all symphonies end in silence, it's equally true that they begin there as well. Silence, after all, both buries and births us, and just as life without the counterweight of mortality would mean nothing, so silence alone, by offering itself as the eternal Other, makes our music possible. The image of Beethoven composing against the growing void, like all clichés, illuminates a common truth: fear forces our hand, inspires us, makes visible the things we love.

But wait. Does this mean that all is well? That the pendulum swings, the chorus turns in stately strophe and antistrophe, the buds of May routinely answer winter's dark? Not quite. We are right to be afraid of silence, to resist that sucking vacuum—however much we depend on it—to claw and scratch against oblivion. The battle is in deadly earnest. And therein lies the joke. Resistance is one thing, victory another.

Left partially deaf by a childhood inflammation of the mastoid bones, Thomas Edison throughout his life embraced the world of silence, reveled in its space, allowed it to empower him; as much as any man, perhaps, he recognized silence as the territory of inspiration and cultivated its gifts. Deafness, his biographers agree, acted like an auditory veil, separating him from the world's distractions, allowing him to attend to what he called his business: thinking.

I mention these facts, however, not for the small and obvious irony—that a man so indebted to silence should do more than any other to fill the world with noise—but to set the context for a scene I find strangely compelling. In June 1911, hard at work on what would eventually become the disk phonograph, Edison hired a pianist to play for him (as loudly as possible) the world's entire repertoire of waltzes. And there, in the salon at Glenmont, either out of frustration at not being able to hear the music to his satisfaction or, as I'd like to believe, out of sudden desperate love for the thing he'd missed (as charged as any of love's first fumblings), the sixty-four-year-old Edison got on his hands and knees and bit into the piano's wood, the better to hear its vibrations. Will Edison's fate be our own? Afloat in the river of sound loosed upon the world by Edison's inventions, having drunk from it until our ears ring, we now risk a similar thirst.

Tacked to the wall above my desk, staring out from a page torn from the back of the *New York Times Magazine,* are the faces of seventeen men and women whose portraits were taken by KGB photographers more than half a century ago, then filed, along with hundreds of thousands like them, in the top-secret dossiers of Stalin's secret police. Over the years, I've come to know the faces in these photographs nearly as well as I know those of the living. I study them often—the woman at the left whose graying hair has loosened from its bun, the beautiful young man at the right, the fading lieutenant at the bottom corner whose cheeks, I suspect, had the same roughness and warmth as my father's— because each and every one of them, within hours of having his or her picture taken, was driven to a forest south of Moscow and executed; because all, or nearly all, knew their fate at the time their pictures were taken; and because, finally, having inherited a good dose of Slavic morbidity (and sentimentality), I couldn't bear to compound the silence of all of those lives unlived by returning them—mothers and fathers, sons and lovers—to the oblivion of yet another archive, the purgatory of microfiche. On my wall, in some small measure, they are not forgotten; they have a voice.

Today, as the panopticon reveals to us, as never before, the agony of our species, the lesson is repeated daily. We read it in the skulls of Srebrenica, growing out of the soil, in the open mouths of the dead from Guatemala to the Thai-Cambodian border, whose characteristic posture—head back, neck arched—seems almost a

universal language: the harvest of dictatorship, properly understood, is not death, but silence. Mr. Pinochet's *desaparecidos* (like
Slobodan Milošević's, or Heinrich Himmler's) are really *los cal-
lados* (the silenced), the snuffing of their voices only the last, most
brutal expression of a system dependent on silence as a tool of
repression. The enforced quiet of censorship and propaganda, of
burning pages and jammed frequencies, is different from the gun
to the temple only in degree, not in kind.

And yet who could deny that silence, though both the means
and end of totalitarian repression, is also its natural enemy? That
silence, the habitat of the imagination, not only allows us to grow
the spore of identity but also, multiplied a millionfold, creates
the rich loam in which a genuine democracy thrives. In the silence
of our own minds, in the quiet margins of the text, we are made
different from one another as well as able to understand others'
differences from us.

In the famous John Cage composition *4'33"*, the pianist walks on-
stage, bows, flips the tail of his tuxedo, and seats himself at the
piano. Taking a stopwatch out of his vest pocket, he presses the
start button, then stares at the keys for precisely four minutes and
thirty-three seconds. When the time is up, he closes the piano
and leaves the stage.

Nearly half a century after it was first performed, *4'33"* rightly
strikes us as hackneyed and worn, a postmodern cliché intent on
blurring a line (between art and non-art, order and disorder, formal
structure and random influence) that has long since been erased.
As simple theater, however, it still has power. Cage's portrait of
the artist frozen before his medium, intensely aware of his allotted time, unable to draw a shape out of the universe of possibilities, carries a certain allegorical charge, because we recognize in
its symbolism—so apparently childlike, so starkly Manichaean—a
lesson worthy of Euripides: art, whatever its medium, attempts to

pry beneath the closed lid of the world, and fails; the artist, in his or her minutes and seconds, attempts to say—to paint, to carve, in sum, to communicate—what ultimately cannot be communicated. In the end, the wedge breaks, the lid stays shut. The artist looks at his watch and leaves the stage, his "success" measurable only by the relative depth of his failure. Too bad. There are worse things.

But if silence is the enemy of art, it is also its motivation and medium: the greatest works not only draw on silence for inspiration but use it, flirt with it, turn it, for a time, against itself. To succeed at all, in other words, art must partake of its opposite, suggest its own dissolution. Examples are legion: once attuned to the music of absence, the eloquence of omission or restraint, one hears it everywhere—in the sudden vertiginous stop of an Elizabeth Bishop poem; in the space between souls in an Edward Hopper painting; in Satchmo's mastery of the wide margins when singing "I'm Just a Lucky So and So." In the final paragraph of Frank O'Connor's small masterpiece "Guests of the Nation," an Irish soldier recalls looking over a patch of bog containing the graves of two British soldiers he's just been forced to execute and observes, "And anything that happened to me afterwards, I never felt the same about again." Such a black hole of a line, dense with rejected possibilities, merciless in its willingness to sacrifice everything for a quick stab at truth.

"Silence," Melville wrote, only five years before withdrawing from writing more or less for good, "is the only Voice of our God." The assertion, like its subject, cuts both ways, negating and affirming, implying both absence and presence, offering us a choice; it's a line that the Society of American Atheists could put on its letterhead and the Society of Friends could silently endorse while waiting to be moved by the Spirit to speak. What makes the line particularly notable, however, is that it appears in *Pierre; or, The Ambiguities,* a novel that, perhaps more than any other in American literature, calls attention to its own silences, its fragility. Offering us a hero who is both American Christ and Holy Fool, martyr and murderer, writer and subject, Melville propels him toward death with such abandon, with such a feel for what Thomas Mann would one day call "the voluptuousness of doom," that even his language gets caught in the vortex: in one particularly eerie passage, we watch the same sentence, repeated four times, being pruned of adverbs, conjunctions, dependent clauses, until it very nearly disappears before our eyes.

There's nothing safe about this brinksmanship, nothing of the deconstructionists' empty posturings. "He can neither believe," Hawthorne wrote, "nor be comfortable in his unbelief." Melville had simply allowed his doubts to bleed into his art. As they will. Having "pretty much made up his mind to be annihilated," he quite naturally took his writing with him.

Reading *Pierre* is an uncomfortable business, akin to watching an artist painstakingly put the finishing touches on his own epitaph. One naturally hopes for a slightly more redemptive vision, a vision that shifts the stress from the inevitability of doom and the triumph of silence to the creative energy these release to the living. Within Melville's own work, we don't have far to look. In *Moby-Dick*, the book he wrote just before *Pierre*, Melville also engineered an apocalypse yet managed to remain far enough away to avoid its pull, to save something, to offer us a metaphor that captures perfectly the tensions essential to our work and our lives. Something survives the *Pequod*'s sinking; though silence may reign over the waters, the vortex eventually slows. The coffin bursts to the surface. And on that coffin are the hieroglyphics of our art.

If one of the characteristics of capitalism is that it tends to shut down options, narrow the margins, then perhaps what we are seeing these days is one of the side effects of the so-called free market: most of the noises we hear are those of buying and selling.

Even the communication between individuals has been harnessed to the technologies that make it possible: to be deprived of the fax machine, the cell phone, the TV, the laptop, etc., is to be relegated to silence. Communication, having been narrowed into whatever can be squeezed into binary code, has been redefined by the marketplace into a commodity itself.

Yet capitalism, we know, always tries to feed the hungers it creates, to confect its own antidotes—so long as the price is right. As the vast silences of the republic are paved over by designer outlets and shopping malls, a kind of island ecosystem remains, self-conscious in its fragility, barely viable. The proof is detectable in any upscale travel magazine: there you will find exclusive spas advertising the promise of silence—no pagers, no cell phones, just the sound of lake water lapping—as though silence were a rare Chardonnay or an exclusive bit of scenery, which, of course, is precisely what it now is.

That silence, like solitude, is now a commodity should not surprise us. Money buys space, and space buys silence: decibels and dollars are inversely proportional. Lacking money, I've lived with noise—with the sounds of fucking and feuding in the air shaft, MTV and Maury Povich coming through the walls, in apartments with ceilings so thin I could hear the click of a clothes hanger placed on a rod or the lusty stream of an upstairs neighbor urinating after a long night out. I've accepted this, if not gracefully at least with some measure of resignation. The great advantage money confers, I now realize, is not silence per se but the *option* of silence, the privilege of choosing one's own music, of shutting out the seventeen-year-old whose boom box nightly rattles my panes.

But if the ability to engineer one's own silence has been one of the age-old prerogatives of wealth, it's also true that the rapidly changing aural landscape of the late twentieth century has raised the status (and value) of silence enormously. As the world of the made, to recall e.e. cummings, replaces the world of the born, as the small sounds of fields at dusk or babies crying in the next apartment are erased by the noise of traffic and *Oprah*, as even our few remaining bits of wilderness are pressed thin and flat beneath satellite transmissions, Forest Service bulldozers, and airplane flight corridors, we grow sentimental for what little has escaped us and automatically reach for our wallets. Like a telltale lesion that appears only on those who are desperately ill, value— even outrageous value—often blossoms on things just before they leave us, and if the analogy is an ugly one, it is also appropriate; the sudden spasm of love for the thing we're killing, after all, is as obscene as it is human. As we continue to pave the world with sound, we will continue to crave what little escapes us, a silence made audible by its disappearance.

Blood on the Tracks

2000

I

Now and again the parallel world of unspeakable things breaks through. A man walks into a schoolyard with a rifle, a taxi leaps a curb, an entire neighborhood folds into rubble. Those directly involved are devoured. The rest, like ruminants slowing to graze once the victim has been culled from the herd, step past the tangle of muscle and bone, the raised, incomprehensible muzzle, and move on. It's been thus since hand in hand we wandered out of paradise.

But if the stories haven't changed, the method of their publication has. Tragedy carries farther in the charged air of the early twenty-first century; death speaks with a louder voice. In Ankara, Turkey, a father unable to get the heavy equipment to move the earthquake rubble listens to his daughter die for two days—and we listen with him. In a town near Albany a mother tortures her three-year-old to death for taking a piece of candy without asking first—and we read about it over our morning Danish. In Pereira, Colombia, a father digs his son out of an ocean of mud, then reburies him in a common grave, and the image of his grief—the mud caked in the hair on his chest, his face broken by weeping—stabs us quickly in the heart on the 7:43 and again halfway through the morning meeting. And so on and so on, ad nauseam, ad absurdum. Soft-shelled and transparent in our vulnerability, we press the button, turn the page, swaddle ourselves in layers of irony. Or try.

Our connectedness, it seems, is engineering something new for us: a need, a hunger, that cannot be satisfied, an existential dilemma fully worthy of Kafka. Unable to ignore the daily parade of bodies left at our doors courtesy of the networks or the newspaper of record or the many offices of the dot-com world, we are being forced to ask the kind of questions—How could this happen? What does it mean?—that we in the West haven't had to ask on such a regular basis since the seventeenth century.

The cracking we hear now is the sound of a great metaphysical wedge being driven into a predominantly materialistic culture. Daily our media drag us to God, force us to inquire after His meaning, then rub our noses in His absence. No one is exempt; even those of us given to wine without metaphor and bread wholly unleavened by faith find ourselves forced back on our convictions, asking again the questions we'd long thought answered.

You say I'm ignoring the multitudes for whom the words "It is God's will" provide all the comfort and explanation necessary? Perhaps, but I am not the first to wonder at the efficacy of answers essentially unchanged since Augustine ("The ways of the Lord are unknowable to man"). The nights grow longer. Let the faithful, like partridge in the Dakota snows, fluff and preen their downy feathers; I wish them warmth and well. This is for the less insulated. We're at aphelion, the farthest distance from the sun. The orbit has broken.

II

At 8:00 p.m. on Monday, May 24, 1999, twenty-three minutes after what would have been sundown had a hard rain not been falling that evening over much of New England, Amtrak's ten-car Twilight Shoreliner, train number 67, departed Boston for Newport News, Virginia.

At 12:35 a.m., after a two-hour delay due to violent weather, it left Providence for stops in Connecticut.

At 2:20 a.m., the Shoreliner, traveling seventy-one miles an hour and carrying 209 passengers, struck five people walking on the tracks near the North Benson Road overpass in Fairfield. Julia Toledo, an Ecuadoran immigrant, and her sons—Angel, six, Carlos, eleven, and Pedro, three—died instantly. The fourth son, José, ten, survived another two days.

By the time José Urgiles de Toledo died at Bridgeport Hospital, the chronology of events leading to the tragedy had been established. Sometime after 9:00 p.m. that Monday night, according to the *Connecticut Post,* Julia Toledo and her sons left the YMCA Families in Transition shelter on Clinton Avenue. The three older boys carried backpacks stuffed with clothes, coloring books, pencils, and Sesame Street dolls. Pedro, too young to walk the entire distance, was probably carried a good part of the way by his mother.

After leaving the shelter unnoticed, the family most likely turned right down Railroad Avenue where it runs below the raised rail bed. No one noticed them; at night the area around Railroad Avenue is badly lit and silent. Several blocks farther down, where crumbling, weedy slopes replace the walls of the raised rail bed, the family climbed a short, steep trail to a break in the chain-link fence and entered the tracks.

To avoid the tilting slope of the rail bed (even for adults, the traprock gravel makes for hard traveling), they must have walked along the tracks for nearly two miles, the older children jumping from tie to tie, until the Shoreliner, sprung from Providence, erased them from the earth.

The facts, of course, were not enough—could never be enough.

In truth, the amassing of details that began immediately following the tragedy was nothing more than a hastily constructed
bridgework—desperate, instinctive—raised by a people with a
long-held faith in the visible world, the world of measurable distances and discernible motivations. A people still accustomed to
assuming that representation confers meaning. That meaning is
there, somewhere, to be conferred.

A map of the scene in the *Connecticut Post,* complete with a
box showing a train with an arrow bearing down on a group of
five black dots, suggested the full depth of the failure. Emergency
workers arriving at the point on the map where the dots and the
arrow met had been "sickened by the carnage," according to New
York's *Daily News.* The train's steel snout, with its red, white, and
blue stripes, was splashed with blood. Scattered over a wide area
were the children's shoes, their torn backpacks, a bloody Bible,
and the Sesame Street dolls the older boys had packed for the
journey. No, no number of facts would suffice. The "what" was not
enough. We wanted a "why." Better still, a "who."

Blame for the tragedy circled the scene, then settled tentatively
on the father. Carlos Urgiles had been abusive, Julia Justiliano, a
crossing guard, told the *Post.* He had threatened to kill his wife,
she said. A year earlier, just before abandoning his family, he had
had to be forcibly removed from the property of Luis Muñoz Marin
School after attempting to steal his own children. The conclusion
was obvious, even welcome: Julia Toledo was on the tracks with
her family that night because she was running from her husband.
Because she was afraid.

This narrative began to crumble when reporters in Ecuador
located Urgiles himself—dark-haired, thin, with the boot-leather
body and the premature stoop of a lifelong laborer—in the small
Andean town of Cojitambo, penniless and three thousand miles
from Bridgeport. Shattered by the news, he told reporters that
his Catholicism had caused tensions with his in-laws (former

Catholics converted to the Church of Jesus Christ of Latter-day Saints) and that they had forced him to leave the country. They had hidden his children before he left. He had gone to Luis Muñoz Marin School out of desperation, he said, not to steal his sons but to try to say good-bye to them. "I have a great pain in my chest," he sobbed during an interview with a TV station in Quito.

The crosshairs now shifted to Toledo's sister, Maria, who owned the Shelton Street house in which Julia and her sons had rented an apartment. Toledo's family, growing tired of the burden Julia and her children imposed on them, reportedly had refused to help with the babysitting. From that point on, the angle of decline steepened. Unable to afford child care, Toledo was forced to quit her job cleaning rooms at Fairfield University. Relations between the sisters deteriorated. Forced to the wall, Julia Toledo moved her family into the shelter.

But blaming Maria and her relations availed us nothing. Even if, as neighbors claimed, Maria had ordered her sister to leave her apartment, had forced Julia, in effect, into the homeless shelter, the fact remained that she had not forced her to leave that night or to climb with her children onto the tracks. We might not like Maria Toledo, might even accuse her, with some justification, of heartlessness, but to blame her would be absurd. Another narrative, straining for closure, ended in midsentence.

As did all the others. Toxicology reports determined that drugs did not play a role. The train was traveling below the speed limit for the area. The engineer was sober, devastated, blameless. Suicide? Maria Toledo's claim that her sister had been unstable was refuted by all who had known Julia in the weeks before she died. The composite portrait that emerged from their descriptions showed a woman full of hope, a survivor, a devoted mother capable of bringing a sense of play and possibility into a life of considerable hardship. All at Caroline House remembered Toledo triumphantly marching in to the Christmas party with a turkey on a platter, her four boys behind her. "Despite her poverty and the problems she had," Sister Maureen told reporters, "she would make a game out of it with her children."

Reconstructions of the event by the Connecticut Department of Transportation and the MTA police also spoke against suicide. Just before they were hit, Toledo and three of her sons were on the south side of Track 3. A fourth son was on the north side. He was crossing over to meet them when the Amtrak blew its horn. Julia Toledo, her three sons in tow, was lunging to save him when they died.

The accident caused one-hour delays of westbound Metro-North commuter trains during rush hour that Tuesday morning and scattered delays that afternoon and evening. By Wednesday, Metro-North service had returned to normal. And yet, for a moment, the tragedy had touched a collective nerve, sent a quick spasm through the virtual community. There was no narrative here, no saving plot. We'd been given a deconstructed poem—all scattered nouns and slippery modifiers, meanings all provisional—held together by nothing more substantial than the fact of its existence and its claim on our attention. An effect without cause, in other words. An apocalypse, writ small. A nightmare of reason and faith alike. It didn't sit well.

The official explainers, trying to make sense of God's purpose in the whole business, gave it a brave attempt, then retreated to safety. "He calls us into relationships with the dispossessed . . . with all those who cry out to God," assayed the Reverend Andrew Garavel, apparently untroubled by the curious notion that the dispossessed should pay for our attention with their lives. Yet at some point even Reverend Garavel at the memorial Mass at Fairfield University, perhaps sensing the porousness of the shelter he offered, was forced to seek deeper cover. The ways of God are unknowable to man, he admitted: "There are things we cannot fully understand. We are a mystery to ourselves and a mystery to one another. If we are that complicated, can we expect God to be any less so?"

To which we might respond, "No, indeed," then counter with a not unreasonable question in return: What good is a God as inscrutable as ourselves, an author whose purpose we can no longer divine? Not much, unless, that is, the Almighty's inscrutability were to conceal a cruelty, a whimsy, as profound as our own.

Earlier in this century, wishing to explore the question of whether human beings could behave without cause, the French novelist André Gide came up with the notion of the *acte gratuit*—the gratuitous act, the motiveless crime. Gide's concept, it seems to me, would have fit Reverend Garavel's Mass perfectly. To dramatize his notion that a crime could be truly motiveless, Gide had a character, out of no malice and for no reason whatsoever, spontaneously push a businessman he'd never met off the train to Brindisi. Risk the analogy. On May 24, God pushed Julia Toledo and her four sons. It's as good an explanation as any.

III

When I first heard Julia Toledo's name, I lived in Leucadia, California—a town rich in bougainvillea and methamphetamine labs—less than a hundred feet from unprotected tracks that ran like a sutured cut from Ensenada to the bay. The trains were as much a part of my life as the eucalyptus trees and the Santa Ana winds. My son had lived with them for nine of his ten years; my daughter, seven, all her life. They'd make us jump—the whistle would blast and hold approaching the Leucadia Boulevard intersection, then bend, ever so slightly, sickeningly, down Christian Doppler's scale—and sitting at the dinner table we could distinguish the deep, tectonic thrum of the big freights from the rapid chatter of the commuters. Sometimes late at night, walking out to the local store for milk, we'd see a double-decker fly by. Well lit and sad, it seemed filled with exiles from an Edward Hopper painting.

Our trains were not the Guthries', father's or son's. Not long after we arrived in California, my wife and I woke to a noise like the howling of a mastiff in a vise. I made it to the window just in time to see our neighbor, a good-natured man who had talked to me just the afternoon before about the advantages of delivering pizza, stagger down the walk and into his apartment. His beloved German shepherd, I discovered, had run onto the tracks. Facing the other direction, gobbling something between the ties, it didn't hear the electric locomotive—so much quieter than diesel—sailing in on the smooth, welded rails, didn't respond to its owner's increasingly frantic calls. The dog wasn't smashed, he told me much later, the horror somehow tied to this one fact above all others; the creature simply disappeared—as though the train were some kind of eraser, the dog he'd known for years but a sketch on a child's slate.

There were other times when the tracks crossed our lives. Some months later a northbound freight slammed into an eighteen-wheeler that had grounded out on the crossing with a concussion so terrific that half a mile away I spilled my coffee all over my desk. I found half the truck like a scissored beetle at the intersection, the other half at the end of a three-hundred-yard trench dug into the rocks and wild melon vines of the rail bed. Seeing how things were, the driver had bailed out and watched from the road as the engineer, trying to stop what couldn't be stopped, rode the train a full quarter mile to the moment everyone knew must come. He lived.

Others did not. Fairly regularly, somewhere along the line, the trains that punctuated the hours of our days passed through men like a stick through an egg: men walking to the canyons to sleep, men thick with tequila, men, like the four who died together one night, playing cards on the ties. I'd seen the warning signs on Highway 5—the stenciled silhouettes not of a leaping deer or elk but of a migrant family running across a road, a man dragging a woman dragging a little girl nearly airborne like the tail of a kite—but the signs were in the wrong place. It was the locomotive, appropriately enough—that grand, nineteenth-century emblem of our imperial reach, our elect status—that killed them. After a day spent moving the Anglos' dirt or muscling trees with hundred-pound root balls into the desert soil, they went down before the iron horse, symbol of God's approbation and love for us, not them. Destiny made manifest.

I knew these things—it would have been impossible not to— and yet there was time enough, life enough, separating one incident from the next, large tragedies from small, that I was able to keep them and the questions they brought with them at bay. My life, the dough of my days, folded them in. Our neighbor became our friend, played with our children, brought another dog home from the pound, and grew to love it. Little boys threw sticks in the trench; dogs peed in it. Eventually the city covered it up. The men who died on the tracks were strangers to me; I knew neither their faces nor their stories.

Julia Toledo's death, though distant, cut closer to home. Like tens of thousands of others, I didn't know she had lived until the day the news, traveling through the threads and ganglia of the nation's web, told me she had died. Three thousand miles away, preparing to move east (my destiny no longer manifest), I heard about her fate, saw her face and the faces of her sons, and felt that in a world of unspeakable wrongs, some manner of crime had been committed. A crime as gratuitous as it was wretched. A crime, like so many others, that demanded a wider reckoning.

I traveled to Connecticut. I walked the tracks at night as the trains came rushing out of the north like great, speeding walls. There was nothing to know, no one to speak to.

IV

During the American Civil War, observers noted a curious fact: the sounds of a battle, clearly distinguishable at ten miles, could be utterly inaudible at two. These weird wrinkles in the landscape were called "acoustic shadows." Modernize the phenomenon, let it expand into metaphor, and you have as good a trope as any for the other America, the one living (below the embankment, behind the Lucky's supermarket) in the very shadow of our prosperity.

I went to Connecticut expecting neither revelation nor redemption. I did not go hoping to experience that frisson of tragedy that can help the emotionally stunted feel alive. Hardly a member of the overclass, I had no specific sin for which I felt the need to atone. I went, I suppose, because certain odd details—the red, white, and blue logo of the Amtrak locomotive, spattered with blood, or the red, white, and blue lettering of the Memorial Day edition of the *Connecticut Post* that reported Toledo's death— seemed to suggest some wider meaning. I went, at least in part, to conduct a kind of inquest, not of the dead but of the land they had died in, to report on what I sensed to be our many sins of omission, committed daily, from sea to shining sea.

I was not unfamiliar with the dark side of American exceptionalism. In the California I had left, entire towns constructed of plastic sheeting and cardboard could be found hidden in canyons only a quick walk from some of the priciest real estate in the Western Hemisphere. Julia Toledo, I realized, had more in common with the migrants who somehow daily emerged from the mud and the manzanita brush, miraculously shaved and cleaned, than she did with the people she worked for. Like them, she had lived in the shadow. Only her death—and that only for a short time— had made her visible.

After midnight the area between Clinton Avenue and the tracks in Bridgeport is not a good place. There is little light. Plywood boards cover broken windows, shattered walls. I walked quickly past a group of men standing by a brick building, then took a right onto Railroad Avenue, a narrow, buckled road with weeds coming through the cracks that runs tight and dark against the brownstone wall of the raised rail bed. I was halfway down Railroad Avenue when the full reality dawned on me: they had walked through this wasteland of abandoned warehouses and vacant lots at almost the same time. I could see them, stepping around the piles of moldering furniture and broken brick and crushed Styrofoam boxes, walking past the papers and trash glued to the wall like seaweed by a tide.

They had been afraid—I knew that now—and their fear frightened me. Back beyond the razor wire I could make out odd, bristling shapes (hills of twisted pipe and scrap lumber) and wondered, for a moment, how they must have looked to children no older than my own. I didn't like Railroad Avenue—the darkness of it, the glass and gravel crunching underfoot—and I knew in my bones they'd been glad to leave it. Compared with what lay behind, the yellow billboard advertising McDonald's bagel sandwiches for breakfast, even the blue railroad trestle in the dark overhead, must have seemed almost welcoming.

I climbed the stonelike steps of the bridgework to the trestle, squeezed through the foot-wide gap between the fencing and the bridge (the three bagels, huge and yellow, now only an arm's length away), and entered the tracks. The traprock embankment made for difficult walking. About a mile down, tired of stumbling, I moved up to the track, and, thoroughly spooked, glancing continually over my shoulder like a man afraid of ghosts, I walked onto the North Benson Road overpass where the accident had occurred.

There was nothing there. Like everyone else, I suppose, I'd wanted a narrative, an explanation. I'd found none. Some measure of guilt—vast, disembodied, cultural—yes. But nothing to explain the magnitude of what had occurred over the North Benson Road overpass on the night of May 24. I picked up a couple of railroad spikes, heavy and crude as Roman nails. The ground seemed to charge with current, and suddenly the train was there, already flying by, gone. I stood for a while in the silence it left behind, then began the long walk back.

V

On Sunday, July 8, 1741, Jonathan Edwards, last of the great New England Calvinists, preached a sermon at Enfield, Connecticut, less than sixty miles from what was then the thriving fishing community of Bridgeport. A spare, almost delicate man, he waited for the knock and scrape of boot soles to still, for the sawing of insects to rise again, and began. His voice that morning, according to an account left by the Reverend Eleazar Wheelock, was level, clearly modulated. He held the small sermon book in his left hand, carefully turning the pages with his right.

The sermon left the audience hysterical. God was angry, Edwards told them, tried beyond all measure. The whirlwind of their destruction would come at any moment, was already overdue; they all—the farmers with the sunburned hands, their stolid wives and frightened children—would be as the chaff on the summer threshing floor.

And he reminded them of the full ferocity of God's wrath ("And the people shall be as the burnings of lime, as thorns cut up shall they be burnt in the fire"), of His eagerness, tempered only by His sovereign will, to make the fallen suffer: "I will tread them in mine anger, and will trample them in my fury, and their blood shall be sprinkled upon my garments, and I will stain all my raiment."

Edwards's sermon that morning contained the only extended metaphor he would ever use, a tidbit of literary history I find strangely eloquent. "The bow of God's wrath is bent," he told the small congregation of weeping sinners, "and the arrow made ready on the string, and justice bends the arrow at your heart, and strains the bow, and it is nothing but the mere pleasure of God, and that of an angry God, without any promise or obligation at all, that keeps the arrow one moment from being made drunk with your blood."

Meaning is made, not discovered, and the materials from which it is cobbled can be very small indeed; a footnote can be the button, the joint, that moves the arm of history. Set in context, made to speak, it can allow the past to touch the present, link the living to the dead. Edwards's bloody metaphor, its point properly honed, should extend to the turn of the millennium. It doesn't. Which is precisely what makes it significant to us.

In 1741, in Enfield, the arrow trembling on the string could both explain our tragedies and terrify us to righteousness. Two and a half centuries later, it can do neither. It is a metaphor, nothing more; a gremlin in a disenchanted world; a spook-house prop. The problem, as always, is the actual blood. It's real enough. And it requires an explanation. A context, a story.

Where do we turn? Lacking God, should we reacquaint ourselves perhaps with His fallen Other? The pagan god gone bad, his horn and hoof retained, his marsh reed pipes exchanged for a pitchfork? It won't do, any more than "fe-fi-fo-fum" or "the better to hear you with, my dear." No, something older is needed, something darker, nearer to the blood. The Greeks' *dia-bollein* (distant progenitor of all things diabolical), for example, meant "to tear apart, to rend."

The force that rends. Perhaps. Something was undeniably torn in Fairfield, a world cut at the root. But it's not enough. No metaphor today can measure up to the thing in itself: the coloring book on the embankment, paging in the wind; the monsters and fairies, half-crayoned in. Neither God nor demon can bear the smallness of the dolls found scattered along the tracks. And that is our problem.

VI

For millennia death stayed close. Life was like a Poussin landscape: tucked to the side, arbored by vines, was a small yellow skull, Virgil's quaint reminder, *et in Arcadia ego*—I too am in the garden—scrawled across the pigment beneath. The memento mori was redundant, of course, possibly cruel; we needed no reminding. We died like midges in October, of infections and colds and tainted milk, and succored ourselves with God, with the knowledge that the causes of our grief, however inscrutable, were after all but His instruments.

Well into the nineteenth century, in other words, we lived in a legible universe, the record of our days—and their meaning—running like a never-ending stream of ticker tape from the mouth of God. The universe was didactic and was to be studied because it was the providence of God in operation. "When a man lookes on the great volume of the world," wrote Puritan divine John Preston, "there those things which God will have known, are written in capitall letters." In seventeenth-century New England, as in the Paris of Louis XIII and his court painter, Poussin, life was the text—a living, breathing allegory—and God was the author.

Something changed. Our lot improved. Death, though still and forever in the garden, was pushed to the margins. And God, reluctantly, went with it. Having washed our hands of blood (dinner now arrived without the quick crack of bone or the "thup" of the stick on the rabbit's neck), having pushed even our own deaths offstage, to the quiet ghettos and discreetly lit reservations deemed appropriate to such unpleasantness, we allowed the myth that gave blood meaning to slip quietly into something like obsolescence. It became, slowly, inexorably, an anachronism: the metaphysical equivalent of the moldboard plow.

So far, so good. Many of us today miss neither the skull nor its apologists, and I, for one, harbor no hidden nostalgia for the golden age of death's dominion or for the architecture of humility and suffering that made it bearable. But, alas, that's not the end of the story. At the turn of the new millennium, appropriately enough, thanks to the wonder-working providences of the communications revolution, death is once again a daily companion. Open the paper on any day of the week, and there is Poussin's skull, set among the harvest of the burgeoning market. Like an icon we can neither override nor delete. Like a boulder in the bitstream. *Et in Arcadia ego,* it whispers—arrogant, insistent—from the columns adjoining the cashmere and the chrome. Et in Zaire. Et in Rwanda. Et in Milwaukee, you fuckers. Turn the page. Delete me.

There's blood on the tracks. A mother and four sons have died in Connecticut. Reflexively, we reach for the myth. But we've forgotten how to read. And we've forgotten how to believe. And the text has gone dark. And the author, whoever he was, if he was, has left.

Necessity and absence are giving birth to something new: a bloodier God, or a truer silence.

Historical Vertigo

2003

I moved to Prague the same time I started doing e-mail: two gestures—or embarkations, I suppose—so perfectly opposed in direction and meaning that I've come to think of them as linked, a kind of metaphysical push-me-pull-you; a subtle rack, on which I, subtly, am being stretched. The first, I want to say, is stone, goes deep, is mute. The second, like helium, surfaces relentlessly, is all gas and fiber-optic chatter. The first is about the endless negotiations between time and place; the second slips these coordinates, by which human beings have always plotted their position, as easily as . . . what? As nothing I have ever known.

A dissonance worth reckoning with, if only because it is inescapable in our age. To spend a winter walking about Prague—before the great river of tourists that begins to rise in March has transformed the city into a giant bazaar, a marketplace almost medieval in its pageantry and babble of tongues—is to bear witness to an essentially ontological conflict. On the one side is being inscribed in stone and plaster and brick, in the continual descent of sediment in whose layers our days, and the days of those who came before us, can be found. On the other is the Internet Café (whose vaulted ceiling was built two hundred years before Columbus) in which being has been, quite literally, disembodied, displaced.

At times, standing on some badly cobbled street in the winter dark, the smell of coal smoke in the air and someone's cell phone digitally chiming the opening notes of the Beatles' "Yellow Submarine," you can almost hear the two forces crashing into each other like tectonic plates, the one going deep, disappearing, buried beneath the wedge, the other rising like air.

I held off until 2003, stubbornly sending and receiving my letters in envelopes, then bent to the prevailing winds. I say bent, not broke. I may yet bend back. In any case, I sent my first e-mail. A questionable friend plugged the machine into the wall (you'll pardon me if I marvel at the ordinary for a moment), showed me how to tiptoe into and out of the labyrinth, and voilà!—there it was—a space in which to compose my note. Feeling oddly unsure of myself, I typed in a "Hello, just testing" kind of message, maneuvered the pointer to the "send" rectangle, and clicked the mouse, which shall forever be the thing with fur whose chaotic nest of lint and cloth and mattress stuffing containing six squirming babies the size and color of lima beans I found in my father's typewriter in the writing shed one April when I was six, but never mind. And my message disappeared.

I'll confess to a certain exhilaration at first. I was the Gettysburg veteran in 1924, all shaky limbs and handlebar mustache, getting into a Model T. I'd sworn I'd never do it. And yet . . . the wind! The speed! So this was the new age I'd resisted so strenuously. It seemed relatively easy, undeniably convenient, faster than a speeding bullet. Often I'd get a reply to my first message while I was still composing the second, an odd feeling, as though the recipient and I had met somewhere in the dark over the Atlantic. I felt very modern, light, unburdened. I could reach out and tap someone on the shoulder whenever I damn well pleased. I could look up the e-mail addresses of people I had never spoken or written to (I didn't have anyone particular in mind) and write them . . . something. Never mind what. Contact! Contact! That was the thing. So what if Thoreau's exhortation had been aimed elsewhere?

While I was waiting for my e-mails to materialize out of the ether, I took long walks through Prague and gravity began to reassert itself. To resist the flooding of the Vltava, the level of the Old Town had been raised by carting in tons of dirt from the countryside, in the process burying the town four meters underground. In some places one could still walk into the basements of buildings and find the outlines of stoned-in windows that half a millennium ago had swung out onto sunlight and rain, onto gardens and streets and courtyards. And something about the soil rising up over the doorstep, the window frame, the sill, burying worlds, moved me. When I passed a construction crew working on a broken water main by the harsh white light of halogen lamps one evening, I glimpsed, beneath the piping, old foundations and ancient sewers made of fist-sized stones and, beneath them, still other, deeper foundations. Everywhere I turned, I saw layer upon layer: stucco walls flayed to brick, brick giving way to stone, stone to a kind of gruel-like mortar. On the Charles Bridge, on the very same cobbles where tourists now bargained for Kafka cups and key chains, the Swedish dead had been piled two meters deep during the Thirty Years' War. At the Church of Sts. Cyril and Metoděj, five minutes from my apartment, the Gestapo had laid out the bodies of the Czech paratroopers who had assassinated Reichsprotektor Reinhard Heydrich. The crypt in which the seven young men had hidden themselves was still there, like a giant honeycomb, smelling of damp and plaster, riddled with bullets.

Strophe and antistrophe. Back at the apartment, the children asleep or reading, I would plug the computer into the wall and wait for the screen to light up. Wait for the menu, click on the icon, listen to the signals dialing for access, press "enter," then "enter" again. I found it difficult to resist. What if something required my attention? And sure enough—I had six unread messages. Or ten. When we went on a three-day trip to Moravia, where the snow in the forests had begun to melt and where we walked for hours listening to the sound of water running under shelves of ice, I returned home to twenty-three! I'd never felt so important in my life.

Of course, the messages I received could hardly be called letters; the majority were something else: notes, afterthoughts, ephemera, doomed to their nanosecond, then floating away in the bitstream. And form followed function, by and large. This was the medium of the present tense, a world of dashes and ellipses, of missing salutations and truncated thoughts, of speed over content, speed over reflection, speed over everything. I found myself answering in kind, tapping out a line or two, getting done, and when I did take the time to write a letter-length message in which I actually described something, or speculated about someone, or recalled some time or other, it seemed forced, even unnatural. Simply put, history did not fit here. I was using the wrong tool for the job, hammering a nail with a putty knife, digging a trench with a file.

We all accommodate the world differently, negotiate toward different ends. There is no universal Greenwich time for the soul. Some buy a new set of golf clubs; others find Jesus. Still others build bombs. My sense of true, of plumb, required a smaller adjustment. I bought a pen. And not just any pen, but a steel-nib pen, meant for dipping, and a good bottle of blue-black ink. And that evening when my wife and I returned from our walk, after I'd read to the kids and we'd put them to bed, I sat down at the kitchen table and wrote a letter. It took a while. The pen blotted or skipped. I dipped too much or not enough. My handwriting, like everyone else's in the world, had gone to hell. I made a mess, smeared ink on my fingers, awkwardly crossed out what I couldn't delete, compensated for afterthoughts with carets and arrows, grew irritated when the ink ran out midthought or midsentence.

But it felt right, somehow. Appropriate. Perhaps even necessary.

I learned how to hold the pen so the ink wouldn't blot, so my *L*s wouldn't disappear on the downstroke. I learned how to dip the pen and touch the rim of the well with the nib just enough to draw the excess. I learned how to sense when the ink was running out, and dip in time. And I grew to love—don't laugh, there is a kind of love we can feel for the things that suit us—the imposed slowness of it, the messy physicality of it, the complicated rhythm of write, dip, touch, think, write. I began to see the beauty of constraint, to appreciate the things it can force from us. I began to understand the shaping force that a less malleable medium can exert on us.

A less malleable medium—it seems a fine metaphor for life. Maybe even a synonym. After all, didn't we, each and every one of us, spend our years shaping the none-too-malleable mediums of opinion and power and love that surround us, and being shaped by them in turn? And weren't we the men and women we were in large part because of how we had responded to the forces around us? How many of the things we did—falling in love, getting married and unmarried, having children and watching them grow at heartbreaking speed—were friction free?

I continued taking my walks through Prague, listening to the sediments settle, like Joyce's snow, over the living and the dead. And I continued writing my letters, both by nib and by byte, trying to understand what it was, precisely, that I found so nourishing about the one and so depleting in the other. Was it the "oldness" of the earlier technology that brought it into alignment with the city I lived in? No. One of the things I found least appealing about Prague was its hawking of its own history, the ubiquitous dates on cups and T-shirts and key rings, the way it kept licking and licking every ribbed vault and architrave until they were raw. An uncritical obsession with antiquity, I knew, could be as much a fetish as the new age's obsession with newness.

But if it wasn't history I was after, what was it then? It came to me gradually, as insights will. I realized that what I found most compelling about the city I lived in was not just its inescapable verticality, the sudden scent of some other century on a street corner at dusk, but its arguments: the weedy battlements above the tennis courts, the fourteenth-century church between the Soviet-era warehouses, the rococo ornamentation on a facade above the KFC. The cobbles rising through the cracked cement.

It was this seething, this dialogue, that I missed in the digital world. E-mail was a done deal. It was efficient. It was pleasant. It was, essentially, commercial. It was like the men and women in the tourist stalls along Pařižská Street, who could say please and thank you and we have a smaller one and here is your Visa card in English and Italian and French and German, but nothing else. It was a conveyor belt, superbly designed to handle compact little parcels of information, disguised as communication. It was the cement.

It's night. The windows are open. The courtyard smells of lilacs and kerosene, *knedliky* and metal. And this is what I believe: that most of us, whether we realize it or not, live in a steel-nib world: slow, messy, full of all-too-visible deletions and clumsy afterthoughts. A Prague of sorts. We may hate it, find it absurd, long for some cleaner place. Perhaps we should. Perhaps it's inevitable that we evolve away from who we are. But it's what's best about us.

Speak, Video!

1993

I

Let me begin with an observation on human nature so generally accepted it borders on truism: identity, both individual and cultural, is defined by one's relation to the past. Whether we resist or embrace the past is relatively unimportant; either way history deals the featuring blow. If that is true, however (and there is overwhelming evidence—both mythic and empirical—that it is), then our ever-increasing ability to freeze time—to embalm the passing moment, as it were—is of vital importance.

Every step in the evolution of technology designed to preserve and store the past—from the mnemonic iambic line to the development of writing, from the daguerreotype to the camcorder—has been a transgression on the territory of private memory. For millennia, after all, the passing of each generation was accomplished by a great dying-off of the past in all its particulars. The sights and smells and sounds of an entire lifetime—transcribeable, if at all, in only the most primitive, partial way—would pass into night with the individual consciousness that had experienced them. To a great extent, the slate was rubbed clean, and each generation could begin the process anew.

That human beings have always fought this recurrent tide is not only true but inevitable. In many respects, I suppose, it is the *desire* to fight it that makes us human. To what extent we should succeed in our fight is another question. We have come a long way very quickly. Although we have been able to freeze visual images since the advent of photography midway through the nineteenth century, we tend to forget that it was not until 1935, for example, that we developed the ability to store information electromagnetically. With that first tape recorder—like beachcombers snatching shells from the surf—we could permanently save a world of sounds and voices from oblivion. Now, at the dawn of the video age, we stand ready to preserve the particularity of physical motion, the fluidity of individual expression, the unique juxtaposition of the aural and the visual.

What our technology has tapped into, obviously, are a number of great and timeless human dreams—dreams so pervasive they border on cliché: to stop the flow of time; to relive moments from our past; to preserve, in ever-greater detail, our private histories; to perpetuate ourselves and those we love. These are things not easily resisted, and already there's a vast and growing library of private moments. With every passing hour, the past takes up more of the present.

I was born on the day the Soviets lofted *Sputnik* into space: technology's child. But sensibilities, like obsolete organs or useless limbs, adapt slowly to new times. Real adaptation occurs over generations, not years or months. My unease over the prospect of vast video libraries of the dead, forever moving and talking and laughing in amber, must be understood for what it is: evidence of a sort of stunted psychic development, an evolutionary case of the bends. I'm not ready; I'm not sure any of us is. All traditions die hard, particularly the old and rooted ones, and at issue here is a cultural tradition as ancient as human consciousness: the tradition of giving over to death what rightfully belongs to it. To put it bluntly, I've lately had cause to wonder whether death *should* have some dominion.

If experience teaches anything, it is that some dreams are best fulfilled slowly and carefully, others not at all. Our free fall into the video age bears watching. Or, to shift to a less ominous metaphor, the game may be fun but the rules are vague and the stakes impressive. What we risk altering is nothing less than the time-honored demarcation between life and death, the quality and the grain of private history, the privilege of memory, the right of revision, the balm of forgetting. A great tinkering has begun. We are playing at the psychological equivalent of genetic engineering, except that *we* are the scientists and our own minds are the frost-proof strawberries, the three-pound mice. None of this should be taken lightly.

II

There are times in every life when the past acquires a particular resonance, when we grow sensitive to sounds and voices normally beyond the range of hearing. The past shades into present always and everywhere, but only rarely do we acknowledge the process; only rarely does some trigger force us to recognize ourselves as citizens of that frontier.

Last summer I spent two weeks carrying the past over a landscape bent on forgetting. In June I spent a rainy afternoon, evening, and night in the basement of my parents' home in suburban Pennsylvania. After forty-six years of marriage, they had gone their separate ways. My mother acted out that most repressed of American dreams and returned to the old country, to streets and courtyards thick with memory, to the smells of cooked cabbage and *knedliky,* to the constant presence of companions both living and dead. My father chose to stay but moved out of the house. The past (an entire basementful) became my ward.

I descended with a chair and a cup of coffee, naively confident that I'd be up before my wife put our son to bed. Eight months and three thousand miles later, I still haven't completely emerged from that basement. Surrounded by the dim bulks of boxes outside the light's circle, I sat up late into the night. Dispersed among the acquired mementos of several generations—the shells and stones and snake skins, the fishing lures and first-grade spellers, the children's clothes stiff and delicate as parchment—were thousands upon thousands of photographs. Some were in boxes and envelopes, others haphazardly stacked in great, curling piles. Pictures in shoeboxes, pictures in jars. A handsome man in a First World War uniform smiled up from the bottom of an old tackle box, his teeth showing white in the shade of a summer oak. I descended and surfaced, regaining the present only to be drawn down again by the next photograph, the next letter or telegram.

Hour followed hour. I struggled with great handfuls of letters, many still in their red and blue *luftpost* envelopes, the pages packed and densely scripted; with shoeboxes full of negatives; with piles and mounds of postcards, many featuring the five-heller stamps of Emperor Franz Josef that dated back to the Austro-Hungarian Empire. Entire lives passed before my eyes. I was reminded of the way clouds gather and disperse in high-speed photography.

The impression made by one postcard remains especially vivid. My great-uncle, a boy of sixteen, was a prisoner of war in Russia. On May 15, 1917, his sister Ludwa wrote him a brief note: "At noon today, Frantik Bacofske arrived and shot himself on their grave. He shot himself in the head but still talked. Before they got him to the hospital, he died. I'll tell you about it in a letter. I don't have time now. Till then, Ludwa."

And everywhere, gloriously random but threading the whole, the photographs—history and geography meshed as arbitrarily as though the entire dusty mass were some grand metaphor of the mind relaxing into second childhood. My mother in 1949, at the

age of twenty-four, overlooking postwar Munich from St. Peter's
Church, the row of buildings to her right ripped open like a torn
honeycomb. My father in 1952, shirtless, a handkerchief on his
head and a bowl of paint in his hand, whitewashing the walls
of some apartment in the slums of Sydney. My mother again,
this time in 1928, a round-faced toddler on a sunny hillside in
Moravia, staring suspiciously at the cameraman. Even me, at fifteen months, all drumbelly and baby fat, walking purposefully
along the edge of some pond in the Catskills, so similar to the
child already asleep upstairs as I write this that I thought for an
instant a current photograph had slipped into these labyrinths by
mistake. My great-grandfather, mustache exquisitely waxed, surrounded by women in white "Gibson girl" dresses—1903.

Each photograph seemed ripe with secrets; each face contained
its own private catalog of fears and desires, of things seen and
people loved and mistakes made. And above it all, carrying the
not-unpleasant odor of old, dry books: the scent of mortality. Lives
rose and fell like bubbles in a vat, and what remained was a tangled
skein of connections, of links and intersections, a thrush's nest in
January.

With the night edging toward dawn, I returned one more
handful of photographs to the carton from which I'd taken them.
The task I had set myself was impossible. I'd done nothing, and in
two weeks we were moving to California, already terribly pressed
for space. The cartons bulked large in the shadows, suddenly mute.
My own past seemed to linger there with them. I turned and
walked up the stairs. It was decided. We'd take them all with us.

Driving west across the country at the wheel of an eighteen-
foot U-Haul, with a car hitched to a tow dolly that made it literally impossible to back up, I was struck by the strange symbolism
of it all. Here I was, after all, like some latter-day Puritan leaving
the Egypt of the past, bound for the promise of a New Canaan.
Westward was heaven, or rather heavenward was the west, as

Henry David Thoreau had put it. I wanted freedom, forgetful-
ness, a new beginning. And yet I, apparently no less than John
Winthrop aboard the *Arabella* in 1630, needed and nourished a
link to the past. My ambivalence toward all those lives curled up
against each other—riding in their envelopes behind me—was, I
suspected, a particularly American sentiment.

The very landscape confirmed this. Everywhere I looked, the
past showed through like the ghostly outlines of wallpaper through
paint. On one hand, the mini-marts and the shopping malls and
the velvet paintings of Indian maidens with Anglo features—what
Melville, in a less egalitarian age, had called "the vulgar caldron of
an everlasting uncrystalizing Present." On the other, signs of a great
instability: Warsaw, Kentucky; Prague, Texas; Paris, Arkansas. The
lesson seemed clear: the past was essential, inescapable. Canaan
could not be Canaan without Egypt.

On our arrival in California, I carried the cartons of photographs one by one to the garage. I stacked them carefully, noting with pleasure that the dry, Mediterranean climate would treat
them well. Already I looked forward to afternoons of sorting and
labeling; I imagined an entire wall of pictures, a sort of pictorial
genealogy, rising like branches into the present. My son would
grow up familiar with faces past. Someday we would add our own.
I slipped the bolt and locked up carefully.

Waking up early a few mornings later, my wife and son still
asleep, I decided to go to the beach. A ten-minute walk down fog-
bound streets, past fences and walls burdened by bougainvillea,
brought me to the top of a wooden staircase that descended like a
fire escape to the sand. I took off my shoes by the water. The tide
was low, the air shot through with mist. Distance seemed nostalgic, hazy with surf. When the tide retreated, pieces of amber kelp
flapped after it like fish trapped in the shallows.

Perhaps because it was all still so new, because habit had not
had a chance to dull my senses to the particular beauty of the place,

I found myself moved by the quiet glory of that morning; by the dark lines of surf rising out of the windless ocean like tired swimmers; by the strange hieroglyphics of gull and tern . . . I knew (as sometimes happens) that many years later I'd remember that morning, that for the rest of my life, some detail—the smell of brine and broken crab, or the particular shade of wetted stone, or the lazy slap of waves—would suddenly bring it back, vivid and strong.

I'm not sure if I noticed him right away or if I only became aware of his presence as I walked. A man, the only figure visible on the shore, stood with his back to me a few hundred feet ahead. To his left the sand rose in loose dunes to the base of sandstone cliffs. He seemed to be watching something—the gulls, I assumed. It was only when he turned toward the ocean that I noticed his elbows were pointed toward the ground instead of out, and that instead of a pair of binoculars, he held a camcorder. I watched him pan slowly across the cliffs, the sand, the ocean—then turn my way. I hesitated, not wanting to ruin the spirit of the piece he seemed so intent on; I assumed he'd quickly turn back to the deserted shoreline. He didn't. Suddenly self-conscious, aware of myself as a subject, I stopped, then turned to look out over the ocean. It was an absurd moment. I'd had no intention of looking out to sea. It had just seemed like the appropriate thing to do under the circumstances. I turned and started back. Pretending to look up at the cliffs, I glanced discreetly over my shoulder. He was still there, filming me as I walked away.

Even then I sensed that I'd just witnessed one of those rare moments that capture a society in transition, a trembling of the cultural chrysalis. It seemed fitting that California—land of the visual "event," end point of a historical process, a culture, and a continent— should have provided the setting.

Over the next few weeks, newly sensitized to their presence, I noticed camcorders everywhere. I saw them at the playground and the beach, at picnics and birthday parties, everywhere. A few blocks from where we lived, I watched a woman taping a young man washing his car. I was struck by all of these images of (in Michael Benedikt's memorable phrase) "a life not really lived anywhere but arranged for the viewing." At times it seemed that Californians, like Chauncey Gardiner in Jerzy Kosinski's *Being There*, preferred to watch.

And it pissed me off. I resented the convenience of it, the faddishness of it, and when a well-meaning neighbor came by with a videotape he'd made of our son playing in the plastic pool on the front lawn, I sat in front of the VCR and resented the sheer genius of it. With little talent, no effort, and no particular feel for the subject, he had fixed an essence no photograph could ever approach.

Resentment, of course, is a symptom. We resent what threatens us. But in what sense was I threatened? It took me some time to realize that what I was arguing for—in some dim, unarticulated way—was the privilege of parents to make their own memories, to order and value and husband them in their own way. The resistance I felt when our neighbor slipped the cartridge into the VCR, I am convinced, was not unlike that felt by the Masai who until fairly recently would smash any camera aimed their way. The tape to me, like the photograph to them, was a transgression on a species of private property. I wanted to protect some sort of visual essence, to prevent an act of theft.

Rationally my response made no sense whatsoever. What was I doing except defending one representation of the past against another? Why draw the line at that particular point? In what way were the photographs in the garage superior to the videocassette in its neat cover, which I'd marked on the spine and slipped like a volume onto the bookshelf? I even had to admit to a certain ambivalence. Watching that twenty-minute tape, I'd experienced an almost supernatural pleasure. Whatever small resentment I'd felt had been overwhelmed at the time by a sort of dumb gratitude. If my neighbor had asked to make the tape beforehand I would have found a way to decline politely. Now that the thing was made, and mine, I'd fight like a badger to keep it.

That same afternoon I carried the cartons back from the garage. I piled them high in a bulky pyramid on the living-room carpet. It was time to unpack.

III

That the home-video library will eventually supplant the photo album seems beyond question. When have we ever been able to resist a new technology? Clearly, a new age—marked by a new relation to the past and defined by our love affair with the camcorder—has already begun. It would seem an opportune time to attempt to recognize the gains and losses. There are quite a few of both.

My case for the photograph is simple: I value it for its very limitations. We are drawn to the absences, the eloquence of what is not shown. This is true for two apparently contradictory reasons: first, because incompleteness invites the imagination (or, in the case of personal material, the memory) to play—to complete the gesture, establish the context, re-create the time and place and voice; second, because consciously or not we respect the humility and acknowledge the accuracy of the incomplete, the unresolved. Every photograph, every novel, every poem and painting carries an aura of mystery, a graceful reminder of our own mortality. And we do what we can to resolve that mystery. It is this dialogue— between things known and unknowable, between memory and death (for what is death but forgetting, writ large?)—that we chiefly love, that makes us human.

The camcorder, by contrast, offers the illusion of completeness; virtually everything—contexts, voices, background noises—has been provided. To all but the most jaded the result is a miracle of representation, but it's a miracle that isolates us in the essentially passive role of observers. There's nothing to do except watch and marvel. What we have before us is the moment past in all its eccentric glory—or at least this is what the video asks us to believe. But of course it's not true. The camcorder does not capture the past; it is simply an exercise in mimicry raised to a higher level. Its success, its undeniable appeal, is the result of its ability to mask the spaces, to hide the gaps behind a more compelling, more seductive facsimile of what was real. The finished product, however, is no more "accurate," no more objective, than the photograph. Both are acts of creative selection.

Every time we determine a border—whether around a photograph, a painting, or a frame of videotape—we are engaging in a more or less arbitrary act of exclusion. We decide what looks good, what "fits," what "belongs"—and what doesn't. We cannot avoid this; it is the nature of the beast. Whether we are snapping a picture or shooting a tape, we are in some sense "making history," and making history is inherently a creative act. This is not to say (as has become fashionable lately) that history itself is an aesthetic construct. History was an empirical fact in time, undebatable as a balled-up fist. Our efforts to *recover* history, however, are of necessity creative. The video confuses the creative approximation with the thing itself, and that is dangerous.

Such confusion is dangerous first and foremost because it makes us lazy. It offers an easy substitute for the work of memory, the labor of reconstructing the past. In the foreword to his great autobiography *Speak, Memory*, Vladimir Nabokov celebrated the effort involved in the process of excavating the distant past: "I revised many passages and tried to do something about the amnesic defects of the original—blank spots, blurry areas, domains of dimness. I discovered that sometimes, by means of intense concentration, the neutral smudge might be forced to come into beautiful focus so that the sudden view could be identified, and the anonymous servant named."

Nabokov's obsession with bringing the neutral smudge into focus—like Proust's need to follow the trail of memories triggered by the taste of a *petite madeleine* and tea, or the hunger of William Carlos Williams for "the strange phosphorus of the life, nameless under an old misappellation"—serves to underscore a common truth: art, ultimately, is archaeology. Our materials, actual or imagined, purely personal or broadly cultural, are mined from the past. Our minds need the blurry areas, the domains of dimness, the way our muscles need resistance.

A photograph offers that resistance. So does a painting or a letter. What drew me to the photographs and postcards in the garage were precisely those areas of ambiguity. Whose was the hand barely visible in a corner of the picture of my mother as an infant? Why was my father smiling as he painted the walls of that tenement in Sydney? What did his voice sound like then? How did he move as a young man? Who was Frantik Bacofske, in the postcard my great-aunt sent to her brother? Why did he shoot himself on "their" grave? Who were "they"?

Out of the vacuum comes the desire and the need for completeness, for narrative. We imagine rain, a late spring, a soldier still in uniform asking the graveskeeper—an old man in a bulky rain slicker struggling to cover an open grave—for directions. The old man is nearly deaf, with great hairy ears like an overgrown fencerow. He runs a wet sleeve under his nose and points to the far end of the yard, then returns to work. The soldier thanks him politely, walks away . . . and so on, following a trail of our own making. Forced to recall or imagine the moment, the situation, the quality of voice, we grow stronger and more familiar with the territory of the past, both real and imagined; we become more capable of naming the anonymous servant or, if need be, creating him anew. In the video age, arguably, all these things required to fill in the blank spots—things like the powers of imagination and memory—will atrophy.

And that's not all. There is another danger in perfect counterpoise to the one I've described. As the camcorder, in its perfection, threatens to do our remembering for us, it jeopardizes the privilege of forgetting—a basic human right. The memory, after all, both recalls *and* erases as the mind requires. And it is not just *our* ability to forget, to reconstruct, to heal, that is at risk here, but history's willingness to let us do so. To the religiously inclined, one of the signs of divine benevolence might be the fact that history invariably washes away the worst. Even horrors, in all but the most extreme cases, begin to blur almost immediately. Pleasures tend to keep their shape, to remain poignant. Forgetting, in other words, whether it is done by us or for us, is an essential kindness. The positive side of time.

Videotape tampers with this, as with so many other things. It disturbs the balance, disrupts the flow. The pleasures it offers come at the price of others, far greater though more elusive. The pain it brings—whether by keeping the dead constantly before our eyes in a sort of suspended animation, or by preserving the mannerisms, the habits, the cruelties best forgotten—is potentially exquisite.

IV

To the charge that I belong to the ranks of the technologically impaired—an anachronism, a throwback mired in a nineteenth-century sensibility—I plead partially guilty. I'll admit that I prefer basic materials: wood or stone. Basic tools: an ax, a pen, a wood clamp. Basic entertainments: conversation, a book between two covers, a musical instrument. In my own defense, however, I can honestly say that I'm not incapable of appreciating the wonders— from gene splicing to lasers—that everywhere crowd in on my attention. I'm not insensible to the benefits and beauties of technology. Faced with major surgery, my allegiance to the wood clamp would quickly fade. And yet, my respect for technological marvels is of the same sort a pre-Columbian tribesman might feel for a gun or an automobile: grudging, suspicious, a product of the head not the heart. I can't help it. No Luddite, I nonetheless keep the crowbar handy.

As near as I can tell, my suspicion springs from my instinctive allegiance to the physical world, to the present moment, to the strengths and limitations of the human mind. I distrust whatever tends to improve or displace them. As far back as 1930, Freud had already noted the technological trend I find so disquieting. "Long ago," he wrote, "[man] formed an ideal conception of omnipotence and omniscience which he embodied in his gods. To these gods he attributed everything that seemed unattainable to his wishes, or that was forbidden to him. . . . To-day he has come very close to the attainment of this ideal, he has almost become a god himself. Only, it is true, in the fashion in which ideals are usually attained according to the general judgement of humanity. Not completely; in some respects not at all, in others only half way. Man has, as it were, become a kind of prosthetic God."

It is as a technological prosthesis—an artificial memory—that I fear the camcorder. I see it as part of a much larger cultural phenomenon marked by a willingness to tamper with the limits of our world, or to replace it altogether. This is not quite as absurd as it sounds. Though they are admittedly primitive, alternate "virtual" worlds already exist. Already it has become possible to move and work, to communicate and accomplish physical tasks, to run and jump—with many of the sensations normally attributed to these activities—in worlds that exist only on a computer screen. At any given moment a spot census would reveal hundreds of thousands, even millions, at work and play in artificial landscapes. And when they return from their journeys, like all travelers, they return only partially. The dominion of the real is everywhere under siege. Most would see this as harmless and fascinating. Perhaps it is, but I'm unable to believe it. I've tried.

All of this has led not so much to a revolution in my lifestyle as to an adjustment in my thinking. My priorities have changed somewhat. Near the top of my list, I believe, would be to live in such a way as be more and more "here," as Thoreau once put it. Have I banished all videotapes from my house? Not at all. Would I accept another, were it given to me? More than likely. Resistance, taken too far, becomes an affirmation. But I would keep the video-tape in its place, restrict it, refuse it the reverence it demands.

Still, it's an uncomfortable position I find myself in, constantly wavering like some red-blooded apostle between temptation and righteous resistance. To paraphrase Nathaniel Hawthorne's de-scription of Melville's "metaphysical wanderings," I'm neither able to believe in the new prosthetic god nor comfortable in my unbelief. The analogy strikes me as apt. Melville spent the majority of his life engaged in a prolonged quarrel with God. I seem doomed to quarrel—instinctively until now, the way an opossum will hiss at a speeding truck—with the new god of technology: a deity and its acolytes intent on a new genesis, a new world marked by a new relation to the past, to history, to reality itself. Hawthorne went on to say that Melville appeared to have "pretty much made up his mind to be annihilated." In my own small way, I too have no choice but to side with the naysayers, the new heathen.

I suspect that on some level, life is a matter of indefensible loy-alties. Sometimes in the evening, after our youngest has been put to bed, I drag my favorite chair—a brown leather wingback, bro-ken and worn—to the wall of pictures still growing in the hallway. Some are hardly larger than a postage stamp. I study the faces—the expressions, the eloquence of caught movements, the gestures of the heart. The air seems full of their presence, thick with their voices and their distant laughter. I like the sound of that crowd, enigmatic as the murmuring of shells. Even the most reserved among them, looking out from their respective windows on the wall, seem glad to see me. And I, for my part, enjoy their company almost as much as I do that of the living.

Eclogue

2008

I

It's a small thing, really.

Every June, soon after the oaks have leafed out over our cabin, a pair of phoebes weaves a small, tight nest under the eave by the door. The nest is quite low, and by holding a long-handled mirror under the slope of the roof we can see the clutch of white eggs glowing there against the twigs and the dead grass and the pocket lint. There's always something hidden and wonderful about this first glimpse: the wavering reflection as I tip the mirror this way and that, searching for the right angle, the glass reflecting down to us the sixty-year-old cedar boards, the moldering supports, and then, like a quick window into another world, like that tiny couple in the mirror in the painting by Van Eyck . . . the nest. This is Act One.

Nearly every year, soon after the phoebes lay their clutch, another, larger egg appears in the nest. It's mottled and lovely, and it hatches first. Thus begins Act Two. The fledgling cowbird that emerges from the egg is grotesquely huge, nearly the size of the adult phoebes themselves. The parents, however, notice nothing wrong; they work frantically to supply that cavernous open beak, that gaping yellow throat, even as their own offspring (if they haven't already been shoved onto the planks of the porch) slowly starve under the imposter's wings.

Act Three: The cowbird chick crams the nest, its wings folded over the sides, absurd as a bear in a bassinet. It grows silky and fat. And then one day they're all gone and the nest is empty. Sometimes I find a desiccated packet—a beak and a few bones, little more—under the nest. Curtain and applause.

One year I carried the cowbird's egg into the woods and threw it against the trunk of a tree, where it made a dark, wet spot.

Another year I didn't notice the egg until after it had hatched. Unable to watch the nestlings starve, I took the intruder out of the nest and then, feeling like a fool, tried to feed it chopped worms and minced bits of largemouth bass with a straw. It died—to spite me, I think—sitting hunched up in a corner of the shoebox like a bitter old man in an ill-fitting suit.

A third year, shamefully, I killed the thing outright like a miniature chicken, though the distress of the phoebes over its disappearance touched my heart. After that I let things alone.

And that's where it stands now, more or less. Some years the cowbird comes and the phoebes' nestlings die. Other years it doesn't, and they live. As it has always been, as it was long before I was around to be troubled by it, so it remains. A cowbird was laying its eggs in a phoebe's nest (this is what I tell myself) when Jamestown was founded, when Christ was a somber lad wandering the streets of dusty Judea, when the Enlightened One, moved by mercy, supposedly threw himself into a pit to feed a starving tiger.

What troubles me about the ritual that plays out under the eave, I think, is my own uncertainty in the face of it. It's a problem. I don't know how to read it. On the one hand, its mute endurance awes me; disturbed by my interference, it simply parts like a stream around a child's finger—for years, if necessary, or decades—until the finger is moved. On the other, though I recognize the play's authority, sense its rightness, I find it difficult to be still. The Sophoclean cruelty of the arrangement, which has the parents dutifully feeding their children's murderer even as their own young, unseen, starve under its wings, gets to me every time. Antiquity and endurance are not quite enough. I can do something, save something now. And yet . . .

And yet, far off, I can hear something whispering that this compulsion to do, to intrude ourselves, to improve on what is— even when wholly well intentioned, *particularly* when wholly well intentioned—is the source of all our troubles. Could it be that one of our most quintessential, even admirable human traits constitutes a richly ironic sin, a sin for which we, in the fullness of time, will be punished? Could it be that the pendulum, having swung over the course of the centuries from humility to hubris in the face of nature's mystery, has reached the top of its arc?

Caught in the pause, neither moving forward nor yet falling back, I do nothing—badly. I sit on my sagging porch reading the *New York Times*, trying to ignore the parents flicking to the nest over my head, their beaks crammed with broken insects and worms, trying not to hear the insatiable screeching of the invader or, worse, the faint asthmatic peeping of the phoebes' brood. I fold the page, snap the crease—turn my mind to the pointless (or pointed) cruelties of men, to which I am accustomed. I stand up. I sit down again.

II

I spend my summers—or the bulk of them—in a four-room cabin by the side of a small pond, immersed in the chanting, rasping, riotous chatter of the natural world, a chatter I adore but cannot understand, a chatter punctuated at regular intervals—as if by an invisible host, tapping his knife to a glass—by death. One day I returned to the shack in which I write to find the makeshift door pushed open and my papers covered in blood and hair. Cleaning up the mess, I discovered a hoofed leg, like a miniature satyr's— caught in a crack in the floorboards.

On a hot, still August morning, walking the road that encircles our pond, loosely, like a necklace on a table, I found a painted turtle crushed into the dirt. An aquatic species, it had obviously come from the water to lay its eggs when the car's tire found it. It was only after I'd gently pushed it into the weeds with my foot so the kids wouldn't see it that it occurred to me that I didn't know if it had died coming from the water or returning to it. I bent down and drew it back out of the grass.

Like all painted turtles, it had been beautiful to the point of tastelessness, the underside of its indigo shell, now broken into unfamiliar continents, a child's swirl of yellows and reds spilling, as if through an excess of sheer joy, onto the soft, phallic folds of the neck. I lay it upside down on my hand. It felt warm, I realized, because it had been in the sun. And though I didn't want to, I slid my fingers into the ugly split in the skin and under the cracked plastron and felt them there: small, smooth, oval. I slipped them one by one out of that wreckage—startlingly white, apparently undamaged—and brought them back to the cabin, where I placed them in an old Thompson Cigar box between two layers of sphagnum moss left over from some gardening venture.

They meant a good deal to me, those five orphans, and over the next few weeks I checked the box often, already imagining the Washington quarter–sized hatchlings—perfect miniatures— scurrying over the moss, the aquarium we would set up for them on the bench, the day in September when, half-grown, they would swim off our palms into the darkness of the lake. Instead they browned, then collapsed, as though something inside them had left. The world has its own imaginings.

That afternoon, carrying the box with its increasingly aromatic cargo into the woods, I noticed for the first time the design on the lid—a seventeenth-century antique map of the Americas, complete with representations of three-masted schooners sailing the *Mare Pacificum* and monstrous cyclones under the *circulus aequinoctalis*. In the lower left-hand corner, inside an ornate frame suitable to a wall mirror, were the words: America: *Nova Tabula*.

In another age, I might have heard the low chuckle of divine mirth, sensed a smile in the fiddlehead fern waving frantically on a windless day. "The *nova tabula* is in your hands, you fool," the wind would whisper to me. "There is no map—read as you may, write what you will."

III

The very notion of an intelligent design, I have to say, is slightly embarrassing—it seems so open-faced and naive, so primitive, so depressingly lacking in irony. It suggests that one has somehow missed the fact that life is now all DNA sequencing and logarithms—wetware, to recall the cyberists' piquant phrase—or worse, that one has bought into one of the religious right's cartoons, which is mortifying.

Since I have little hipness to lose, I'll confess it straight out: intelligent design is a notion, a myth—all right, a theology—I've always been attracted to. Unapologetically in love with both the natural world and the written page (between which I sense all manner of linkage, both of which seem to me to be fading from our lives, to our inestimable loss), most at home in myself when I am navigating one or the other, I've found myself wishing at times that on some level it could all be true. Not that Toto might reveal to us at long last the benevolent, white-haired wizard behind the curtain, but something . . . subtler: that we could glimpse the wisdom behind it all, sense, even if momentarily, the pattern in the carpet. How glorious it would be to feel the key turn, to be able to enter the culture of things outside of us, to understand not only the *what* of the universe, but the *why*. To read the slow rain of rising trout, or comprehend—really comprehend—the shocking orange of fungus, labial and exquisite, shining on the underside of a rotting log. To grasp the intent and the glory, the slow fire of life, behind them.

It's a fantasy with a long pedigree. For countless millennia, after all, like three-year-olds who can't read but nonetheless turn the pages, move their lips, we imagined meaning, a narrative, agency. And since everything ultimately has to be about us, the story we imposed on nature was largely our own. The agency behind the screen had not only to resemble us but to care about our welfare. It's almost touching, this presumption. Knowing nothing, we assumed all. Nature became our mirror, our metaphor bank. The cruel sun? The spendthrift weed? Nature was the vehicle; we were the tenor—always. For millennia, and well into the nineteenth century, we read the world metaphorically, much as a Freudian psychoanalyst might read our gestures and verbal slips as clues to the workings of the unconscious. The visible world was a system of signs, pointing to some deeper, hidden actor, who was communicating with us. The cigar was never just a cigar.

It didn't work, of course. The cigar, it turned out, was just a cigar; the sand flea just a sand flea. Nature was not "a grave," "a kind parent," "a merciless stepmother." It didn't "abhor a vacuum," or "the old." Alas, it didn't abhor anything at all. It just went on, perfectly. If nature was a story, it was a new kind of story: plotless, endless, at once both circular and linear, so vast it seemed not to move at all—a millennium hand, an eon hand—yet everywhere seething with a strange and wondrous energy, telling over and over of two great armies folding into one another without rancor or victory . . . we couldn't grasp it.

So we made up our own, more suited to us. And when our made-up story no longer satisfied us, round about the seventeenth century, we decided to take the book apart. Thus, science. As if untying the volume's signatures and teasing apart the paper's weave could reveal something, some wisdom; could teach us, at long last, our place.

Eventually, rounding the curve of the second millennium *antes deum,* the majority of us simply lost interest in the game. We had outgrown childish things. The Other had nothing to do with us. Starting in the industrialized West, we migrated indoors, into mediated environments from which the natural world in all its mystery had been seamlessly removed. We were enough for ourselves. We exchanged "information." We worried about our equity. We spent large portions of our lives watching people we didn't know pretending to be living lives that were not their own. The high wind tossing the continents of trees, the paper wasp tending its soft, masticated nest, the blossom trembling in the sun—these had nothing to do with us. The Other had become merely other— an afterthought, an irrelevance. If it got in our way, or troubled our oversensitive skin, we killed it. If it didn't work the way we wanted, we shaped it to our needs. Wonder? What was there to wonder at?

It occurs to me, though, that our inability to read the Book of Nature—and yes, I intend that uppercase *N* in all its Romantic glory—doesn't necessarily mean there is no book to be read, only that we can't read it; that the stories we've told and the tools we've developed to disarticulate it and the indifference we've cultivated to make it go away won't do. That we need something different. Why? Because the text still matters, whether we can decipher it or not. Because, as seems increasingly clear, unless we reach some proper accommodation with nature, show it a bit of respect, admit our ignorance of it, it will bury us with as little fanfare as night follows day: the evolutionary tide of a billion years will wash over us and recede; a few ticks of the clock hand, and the scars we've made will heal; a paper wasp, moving in the shadow of Lincoln's lower lip, will tend its soft, masticated nest. Which would be a shame; I've grown fond of our maudlin, murderous tribe.

IV

Seen through the other end of the telescope, from the kind of distance that confers clarity, one thing seems certain: we have not yet found the language with which to front the world we inhabit, a world that has worked superbly, if life is the proof, for unfathomable time; a world that continues to hold us—despite the din of our distractions—precisely the way a nest holds an egg. We have not even begun to learn this language; its alphabet is a mystery, its declensions unknown.

There are times, sitting up to my chin in a warm pond watching a damselfly the precise iridescent green of cheap tinsel perch on a spear of weed protruding above the water, feeling the velvety sides of the bullhead catfish bumping against my feet, when I can almost feel it. A genius. A music just beyond my range of hearing. The surface film, cooking in the August sun, stretches before my eyes, a teeming graveyard of mayflies and midges and tiny, ivory-white moths, a macabre and gorgeous litter of wings and legs and antennae, of pale exoskeletons like comic-book armor and lime-green duckweed. Twenty feet out, I can make out the dull glint of a dead bluegill. Water striders and dragonfly larvae move over and through this mat, this mulch. Organisms I know nothing about—a thousand to a bottle cap—zip and spin in every palmful of water. Something is swirling now beneath the dead bluegill and the fish jerks and then rises to the surface again. And I think to myself: This is beyond us. Only reverence is appropriate here.

V

On a still July afternoon two summers ago, a neighbor called to say that he'd found a baby rabbit in an open field by his woodshed. There was no nest in evidence, no mother. It appeared to be starving. Knowing my daughter's willingness to serve as nursemaid (or priest, if necessary) to any and all, he thought she might take it in.

We walked over together to find a baby cottontail, some weeks old, crouched in the corner of a book carton. It was smaller than a man's fist. It had impossibly soft brown fur and strangely sentient brown eyes and wheat-pale whiskers that moved whenever its nose twitched, which was often. When my daughter picked it up, it sat perfectly still in her hands and twitched its rubbery little nose. By the time we'd carried the carton back to our cabin, it had a name.

Winston died three days later. He seemed to be doing well the first day, greedily suckling warm milk out of the eyedropper, wetting his rabbit chin, but by the second morning something was clearly wrong. A terrible stiffness had set in, as if his spine had curved and solidified. His big hind legs, with their reversed rabbit knees, twitched and kicked spasmodically. We took Winston to one of those Good Samaritans who specialize in animal recovery at their own expense, who told us there was nothing we could have done, that baby cottontails were among the most delicate of commonly found creatures.

My daughter, who has grown up in the natural world and thus understands—perhaps better than I—that death, too, is in the picture, buried him along with the dragonflies and the voles and the chipmunks and the cowbird I'd tried to nurse in the clearing behind the second oak.

I wanted to say something, for all three of us, but what could I say? Science couldn't help me here—it spoke a different language, a language washed clean of sentiment and pain. Christ couldn't help me much either. I could have said something, I suppose, about God's plan, but I really had no idea what God's plan might have been in paralyzing Winston, and so, fighting the slightly absurd tightening in my throat, I said that I didn't know why Winston had died and that I was very sorry for it and that we can't always

understand why things happen but that life was all around us—
that there were cottontails at that moment along the edge of the
meadow—so something had to be working right. Something to
that effect. Then we read aloud, as we always do, James Dickey's
"Heaven of Animals." It's a good poem, and it was just good
enough.

That pain. I wondered about it then; wonder about it still.
What was it I mourned, precisely? Not just this creature, or this
creature alone. Not just his leaf-soft ears, or the inward curl of his
front paws, or his mute distress—which seemed obvious enough
by the second morning—but something else as well. Time, maybe.
"Time robs us of all, even of memory," Virgil reminds us in the
Eclogues, his vision of a perfect, haunted world. But whose time? A
rich vein of self-regard, I began to suspect—and self-indulgence,
maybe—ran beneath my sorrow. What Winston called to my attention that afternoon—the impatient clink of the knife on glass—
was death itself. My own, of course (the inevitability of which has
always struck me as distinctly unfair, and somewhat unlikely), but
much more so, that of the little girl next to me, whose life means
more to me than anything else, and whose own mortality . . . it's a
thought I touch like a red-hot oven.

And suddenly I'm there—on the border of acceptance. Of
deference. Perhaps even of wisdom. On this side of the line is
everything eternal; the vast tide of life breathing in and out, endlessly. Beyond it—marked by a running stream, a stand of trees,
a thousand miles of wire—is the territory of love. And I'll step
across it every time.

REFUTATIONS

Quitting the Paint Factory

2004

*Love yields to business. If you seek a way
out of love, be busy; you'll be safe, then.*
—OVID, *REMEDIA AMORIS*

I distrust the perpetually busy, always have. The frenetic ones spinning in tight little circles like poisoned rats. The slower ones, grinding away their fourscore and ten in righteousness and pain. They are the soul-eaters.

When I was young, my parents read me Aesop's fable "The Ant and the Grasshopper," wherein, as everyone knows, the grass-hopper spends the summer making music in the sun while the ant toils with his fellow Formicidae. Winter comes, as winters will, and the grasshopper, who hasn't planned ahead and who doesn't know what a 401(k) is, has run out of luck. When he shows up at the ants' door, carrying his fiddle, the ant asks him what he was doing all year: "I was singing, if you please," the grasshopper re-plies, or something to that effect. "You were singing?" says the ant. "Well, then, go and sing." And perhaps because I sensed, even then, that fate would someday find me holding a violin or a manuscript at the door of the ants, my antennae frozen and my bills overdue, I

97

confounded both Aesop and my well-meaning parents, and bore away the wrong moral. That summer, many a windblown grasshopper was saved from the pond, and many an anthill inundated under the golden rain of my pee.

I was right.

In the lifetime that has passed since Calvin Coolidge gave a speech to the American Society of Newspaper Editors in which he famously proclaimed that "the chief business of the American people is business," the dominion of the ants has grown enormously. Look about: The business of business is everywhere and inescapable; the song of the buyers and the sellers never stops; the term *workaholic* has been folded up and put away. We have no time for our friends or our families, no time to think or to make a meal. We're moving product, while the soul drowns like a cat in a well.*

A resuscitated orthodoxy, so pervasive as to be nearly invisible, rules the land. Like any religion worth its salt, it shapes our world in its image, demonizing if necessary, absorbing when possible. Thus has the great sovereign territory of what Nabokov called "unreal estate," the continent of invisible possessions from time to talent to contentment, been either infantilized, rendered unclean, or translated into the grammar of dollars and cents. Thus has the great wilderness of the inner life been compressed into a median strip by the demands of the "real world," which of course is anything but. Thus have we succeeded in transforming even ourselves into bipedal products, paying richly for seminars that teach us how

---

* "I think that there is far too much work done in the world," Bertrand Russell observed in his famous 1932 essay "In Praise of Idleness," adding that he hoped to "start a campaign to induce good young men to do nothing." He failed. A year later, National Socialism, with its cult of work (think of all those bronzed young men in Leni Riefenstahl's *Triumph of the Will* throwing cordwood to each other in the sun), flared in Germany.

to market the self so it may be sold to the highest bidder. Or perhaps "down the river" is the phrase.

Ah, but here's the rub: idleness is not just a psychological necessity, requisite to the construction of a complete human being; it constitutes as well a kind of political space, a space as necessary to the workings of an actual democracy as, say, a free press. How does it do this? By allowing us time to figure out who we are, and what we believe; by allowing us time to consider what is unjust, and what we might do about it. By giving the inner life (in whose precincts we are most ourselves) its due. Which is precisely what makes idleness dangerous. All manner of things can grow out of that fallow soil. Not for nothing did our mothers grow suspicious when we had "too much time on our hands." They knew we might be up to something. And not for nothing did we whisper to each other, when we *were* up to something, "Quick, look busy."

Mother knew instinctively what the keepers of the castles have always known: that trouble—the kind that might threaten the symmetry of a well-ordered garden—needs time to take root. Take away the time, therefore, and you choke off the problem before it begins. Obedience reigns, the plow stays in the furrow; things proceed as they must. Which raises an uncomfortable question: Could the Church of Work—which today has Americans aspiring to sleep deprivation the way they once aspired to a personal knowledge of God—be, at base, an antidemocratic force? Well, yes. James Russell Lowell, that nineteenth-century workhorse, summed it all up quite neatly: "There is no better ballast for keeping the mind steady on its keel, and saving it from all risk of crankiness, than business."

Quite so. The mind, however, particularly the mind of a citizen in a democratic society, is not a boat. Ballast is not what it needs, and steadiness, alas, can be a synonym for stupidity, as our current administration has so amply demonstrated. No, what the democratic mind requires, above all, is time; time to consider its options. Time to develop the democratic virtues of independence, orneriness, objectivity, and fairness. Time, perhaps (to sail along with Lowell's leaky metaphor for a moment), to ponder the course our unelected captains have so generously set for us, and to consider mutiny when the iceberg looms.

Which is precisely why we need to be kept busy. If we have no time to think, to mull, if we have no time to piece together the sudden associations and unexpected, midshower insights that are the stuff of independent opinion, then we are less citizens than cursors, easily manipulated, vulnerable to the currents of power.

But I have to be careful here. Having worked all of my adult life, I recognize that work of one sort or another is as essential to survival as protein, and that much of it, in today's highly bureaucratized, economically diversified societies, will of necessity be neither pleasant nor challenging nor particularly meaningful. I have compassion for those making the most of their commute and their cubicle; I just wish they could be a little less cheerful about it. In short, this isn't about us so much as it is about the zeitgeist we live and labor in, which, like a cuckoo taking over a thrush's nest, has systematically shoved all the other eggs of our life, one by one, onto the pavement. It's about illuminating the losses.

We're enthralled. I want to disenchant us a bit, draw a mustache on the boss.

Infinite Bustle

I'm a student of the narrowing margins. And their victim, to some extent, though my capacity for sloth, my belief in it, may yet save me. Like some stubborn heretic in fifth-century Rome, still offering gifts to the spirit of the fields even as the priests sniff about the *tempa* for sin, I daily sacrifice my bit of time. The pagan gods may yet return. Constantine and Theodosius may die. But the prospects are bad.

In Riverside Park in New York City, where I walk these days, the legions of "weekend nannies" are growing, setting up a play date for a ten-year-old requires a feat of near-Olympic coordination, and the few, vestigial, late-afternoon parents one sees, dragging their wailing progeny by the hand or frantically kicking a soccer ball in the fading light, have a gleam in their eyes I find frightening. No outstretched legs crossed at the ankles, no arms draped over the back of the bench. No lovers. No behatted old men, arguing. Between the slide and the sandbox, a very fit young man in his early thirties is talking on his cell phone while a two-year-old with a trail of snot running from his nose tugs on the seam of his corduroy pants. "There's no way I can pick it up. Because we're still at the park. Because we just got here, that's why."

It's been one hundred and forty years since Thoreau, who itched a full century before everyone else began to scratch, complained that the world was increasingly just "a place of business. What an infinite bustle!" he groused. "I am awakened almost every night by the panting of the locomotive. It interrupts my dreams. There is no Sabbath. It would be glorious to see mankind at leisure for once. It is nothing but work, work, work." Little did he know. Today the roads of commerce, paved and smoothed, reach into every nook and cranny of the republic; there is no place apart, no place where we would be shut of the drone of that damnable traffic. Today we, quite literally, live to work. And it hardly matters what kind of work we do; the process justifies the ends. Indeed, at times it seems there is hardly an occupation, however useless or humiliating or downright despicable, that cannot at least in part be redeemed by our obsessive dedication to it: "Yes, Ted sold shoulder-held Stingers to folks with no surname, but he worked so *hard!*"

Not long ago, at the kind of dinner party I rarely attend, I made the mistake of admitting that I not only liked to sleep but liked to get at least eight hours a night whenever possible, and that nine would be better still. The reaction—a complex Pinot Noir of nervous laughter displaced by expressions of disbelief and condescension—suggested that my transgression had been, on some level, a political one. I was reminded of the time I'd confessed to Roger Angell that I did not much care for baseball.

My comment was immediately rebutted by testimonials to sleeplessness: two of the nine guests confessed to being insomniacs; a member of the Academy of Arts and Letters claimed indignantly that she couldn't remember when she had *ever* gotten eight hours of sleep; two other guests declared themselves grateful for five or six. It mattered little that I'd arranged my life differently, and accepted the sacrifices that arrangement entailed. Eight hours! There was something willful about it. Arrogant, even. Suitably chastened, I held my tongue, and escaped alone to tell Thee.

Increasingly, it seems to me, our world is dividing into two kinds of things: those that aid work, or at least represent a path to it, and those that don't. Things in the first category are good and noble; things in the second aren't. Thus, for example, education is good (as long as we don't have to listen to any of that "end in itself" nonsense) because it will presumably lead to work. Thus playing the piano or swimming the 100-yard backstroke are good things for a fifteen-year-old to do *not* because they might give her some pleasure but because rumor has it that Yale is interested in students who can play Chopin or swim quickly on their backs (and a degree from Yale, as any fool knows, can be readily converted to work).

Point the beam anywhere, and there's the God of Work, busily trampling out the vintage. Blizzards are bemoaned because they keep us from getting to work. Hobbies are seen as either ridiculous or self-indulgent because they interfere with work. Longer school days are all the rage (even as our children grow demonstrably stupider), not because they make educational or psychological or any other kind of sense but because keeping kids in school longer makes it easier for us to work. Meanwhile, the time grows short, the margin narrows; the white spaces on our calendars have been inked in for months. We're angry about this, upset about that, but who has the time to do anything anymore? There are those reports to report on, memos to remember, e-mails to deflect or delete. They bury us like snow.

The alarm rings and we're off, running so hard that by the time we stop we're too tired to do much of anything except nod in front of the TV, which, like virtually all the other voices in our culture, endorses our exhaustion, fetishizes and romanticizes it, and, by daily adding its little trowelful of lies and omissions, helps cement the conviction that not only is this how our three score and ten must be spent but that the transaction is both noble and necessary.

Ka-Chink!

Time may be money (though I've always resisted that loathsome platitude, the alchemy by which the very gold of our lives is transformed into the base lead of commerce), but one thing seems certain: money eats time. Forget the visions of sanctioned leisure: the view from the deck in St. Moritz, the wafer-thin TV. Consider the price.

Sometimes money costs too much. And at the beginning of the millennium, in this country, the cost of money is well on the way to bankrupting us. We're impoverishing ourselves, our families, our communities—and yet we can't stop ourselves. Worse, we don't want to.

Seen from the right vantage point, there's something wonderfully animistic about it. The god must be fed; he's hungry for our hours, craves our days and years. And we oblige. Every morning (unlike the good citizens of Tenochtitlán, who at least had the good sense to sacrifice others on the slab) we rush up the steps of the ziggurat to lay ourselves down. It's not a pretty sight.

Then again, we've been well trained. And the training never stops. In a recent ad in the *New York Times Magazine,* paid for by an outfit named Wealth and Tax Advisory Services, Inc., an attractive young woman in a dark business suit is shown working at her desk. (She may be at home, though these days the distinction is moot.) On the desk is a cup, a cell phone, and an adding machine. Above her right shoulder, just over the blurred sofa and the blurred landscape on the wall, are the words "Successful entrepreneurs work continuously." The text below explains: "The challenge to building wealth is that your finances grow in complexity as your time demands increase."

The ad is worth disarticulating, it seems to me, if only because some version of it is beamed into our cerebral cortex a thousand times a day. What's interesting about it is not only what it says but what it so blithely assumes. What it says, crudely enough, is that in order to be successful, we must not only work but work *continuously;* what it assumes is that time is inversely proportional to wealth: our time demands will increase the harder we work and the more successful we become. It's an organic thing; a law, almost. Fish gotta swim and birds gotta fly, you gotta work like a dog till you die.

Am I suggesting then that Wealth and Tax Advisory Services, Inc., spend $60,000 for a full-page ad in the *New York Times Magazine* to show us a young woman at her desk writing poetry? Or playing with her kids? Or sharing a glass of wine with a friend, attractively thumbing her nose at the acquisition of wealth? No. For one thing, the folks at Wealth and Tax etc. are simply doing what's in their best interest. For another, it would hardly matter if they did show the woman writing poetry, or laughing with her children, because these things, by virtue of their placement in the ad, would immediately take on the color of their host; they would simply be the rewards of working almost continuously.

What I am suggesting is that just as the marketplace has co-opted rebellion by subordinating politics to fashion, by making anger chic, so it has quietly underwritten the idea of leisure, in part by separating it from idleness. Open almost any magazine in America today and there they are: the ubiquitous tanned-and-toned twenty-somethings driving the $70,000 fruits of their labor; the moneyed-looking men and women in their healthy sixties (to give the young something to aspire to) tossing Frisbees to Irish setters or tying on flies in midstream or watching sunsets from their Adirondack chairs.

Leisure is permissible, we understand, because it costs money; idleness is not, because it doesn't. Leisure is focused; whatever thinking it requires is absorbed by a certain task: sinking that putt, making that cast, watching that flat-screen TV. Idleness is unconstrained, anarchic. Leisure—particularly if it involves some kind of high-priced technology—is as American as a Fourth of July barbecue. Idleness, on the other hand, has a bad attitude. It doesn't shave; it's not a member of the team; it doesn't play well with others. It thinks too much, as my high school coach used to say. So it has to be ostracized.*

With idleness safely on the reservation, the notion that leisure is necessarily a function of money is free to grow into a truism. "Money isn't the goal. Your goals, that's the goal," reads a recent ad for Citibank. At first glance, there's something appealingly subversive about it. Apply a little skepticism, though, and the implicit message floats to the surface: And how else are you going to

---

* Or put to good use. The wilderness of association we enter when we read, for example, is one of the world's great domains of imaginative diversity: a seedbed of individualism. What better reason to pave it, then, to make it an accessory, like a personal organizer, a surefire way of raising your SAT score, or improving your communication skills for that next interview? You say you like to read? Then don't waste your time; put it to work. Order *Shakespeare in Charge: The Bard's Guide to Leading and Succeeding on the Business Stage*, with its picture of the bard in a business suit on the cover.

reach those goals than by investing wisely with us? Which suggests that, um, money is the goal, after all.

The Church of Work

There's something un-American about singing the virtues of idleness. It is a form of blasphemy, a secular sin. More precisely, it is a kind of latter-day antinomianism, as much a threat to the orthodoxy of our day as Anne Hutchinson's desire 350 years ago to circumvent the Puritan ministers and dial God direct. Hutchinson, we recall, got into trouble because she accused the Puritan elders of backsliding from the rigors of their theology and giving in to a Covenant of Works, whereby the individual could earn his all-expenses-paid trip to the pearly gates through the labor of his hands rather than solely through the grace of God. Think of it as a kind of frequent-flier plan for the soul.

The analogy to today is instructive. Like the New England clergy, the Religion of Business—literalized, painfully, in books like *Jesus, CEO*—holds a monopoly on interpretation; it sets the terms, dictates value.* Although today's version of the Covenant of Works has substituted a host of secular pleasures for the idea of heaven, it too seeks to corner the market on what we most desire, to suggest that the work of our hands will save us. And we believe. We believe across all the boundaries of class and race and ethnicity that normally divide us; we believe in numbers that dwarf those of the more conventionally faithful. We repeat the daily catechism, we sing in the choir. And we tithe, and keep on tithing, until we are spent.

It is this willingness to hand over our lives that fascinates and appalls me. There's such a lovely perversity to it; it's so wonder-

---

* In this new lexicon, for example, *work* is defined as the means to wealth; *success*, as a synonym for it.

fully counterintuitive, so very Christian: You must empty your pockets, turn them inside out, and spill out your wife and your son, the pets you hardly knew, and the days you simply missed altogether watching the sunlight fade on the bricks across the way. You must hand over the rainy afternoons, the light on the grass, the moments of play and of simply being. You must give it up, all of it, and by your example teach your children to do the same, and then—because even this is not enough—you must train yourself to believe that this outsourcing of your life is both natural and good. But even so, your soul will not be saved.

The young, for a time, know better. They balk at the harness. They do not go easy. For a time they are able to see the utter sadness of subordinating all that matters to all that doesn't. Eventually, of course, sitting in their cubicle lined with *New Yorker* cartoons, selling whatever it is they've been asked to sell, most come to see the advantage of enthusiasm. They join the choir and are duly forgiven for their illusions. It's a rite of passage we are all familiar with. The generations before us clear the path; Augustine stands to the left, Freud to the right. We are born into death, and die into life, they murmur; civilization will have its discontents. The sign in front of the Church of Our Lady of Perpetual Work confirms it. And we believe.

All of which leaves only the task of explaining away those few miscreants who out of some inner weakness or perversity either refuse to convert or who go along and then, in their thirty-sixth year in the choir, say, abruptly abandon the faith. Those in the first category are relatively easy to contend with; they are simply losers. Those in the second are a bit more difficult; their apostasy requires something more . . . dramatic. They are considered mad.

In one of my favorite anecdotes from American literary history (which my children know by heart, and which in turn bodes poorly for their futures as captains of industry), the writer Sherwood

Anderson found himself, at the age of thirty-six, the chief owner and general manager of a paint factory in Elyria, Ohio. Having made something of a reputation for himself as a copywriter in a Chicago advertising agency, he'd moved up a rung. He was on his way, as they say, a businessman in the making, perhaps even a tycoon in embryo. There was only one problem: he couldn't seem to shake the notion that the work he was doing (writing circulars extolling the virtues of his line of paints) was patently absurd, undignified; that it amounted to a kind of prison sentence. Lacking the rationalizing gene, incapable of numbing himself sufficiently to make the days and the years pass without pain, he suffered and flailed. Eventually he snapped.

It was a scene he would revisit time and again in his memoirs and fiction. On November 27, 1912, in the middle of dictating a letter to his secretary ("The goods about which you have inquired are the best of their kind made in the . . ."), he simply stopped. According to the story, the two supposedly stared at each other for a long time, after which Anderson said, "I have been wading in a long river and my feet are wet," and walked out. Outside the building he turned east toward Cleveland and kept going. Four days later he was recognized and taken to a hospital suffering from exhaustion.

Anderson claimed afterward that he had encouraged the impression that he might be cracking up in order to facilitate his exit, to make it comprehensible. "The thought occurred to me that if men thought me a little insane they would forgive me if I lit out," he wrote, and though we will never know for sure if he suffered a nervous breakdown that day (his biographers have concluded that he did) or only pretended to one, the point of the anecdote is elsewhere: real or feigned, nothing short of madness would do for an excuse.

Anderson himself, of course, was smart enough to recognize the absurdity in all this, and to use it for his own ends; over the years that followed, he worked his escape from the paint factory into a kind of parable of liberation, an exemplar for the young men of his age. It became the cornerstone of his critique of the emerging business culture: to stay was to suffocate, slowly; to escape was to take a stab at "aliveness." What America needed, Anderson argued, was a new class of individuals who "at any physical cost to themselves and others" would "agree to quit working, to loaf, to refuse to be hurried or try to get on in the world."

"To refuse to be hurried or try to get on in the world." It sounds quite mad. What would we do if we followed that advice? And who would we be? No, better to pull down the blinds, finish that sentence. We're all in the paint factory now.

Clearing Brush

At times you can almost see it, this flypaper we're attached to, this mechanism we labor in, this delusion we inhabit. A thing of such magnitude can be hard to make out, of course, but you can rough out its shape and mark its progress, like Claude Rains's Invisible Man, by its effects: by the things it renders quaint or obsolete, by the trail of discarded notions it leaves behind. What we're leaving behind today, at record pace, is whatever belief we might once have had in the value of unstructured time: in the privilege of contemplating our lives before they are gone, in the importance of uninterrupted conversation, in the beauty of play. In the thing in itself—unmediated, leading nowhere. In the present moment.

Admittedly, the present—in its ontological, rather than consumerist, sense—has never been too popular on this side of the Atlantic; we've always been a finger-drumming, restless bunch, suspicious of jawboning, less likely to sit at the table than to grab a quick one at the bar. Whitman might have exhorted us to loaf and invite our souls, but that was not an invitation we cared to extend, not unless the soul played poker, ha, ha. No sir, a Frenchman might invite his soul. One expected such things. But an American? An

American would be out the swinging doors and halfway to tomorrow before his silver dollar had stopped ringing on the counter.

I was put in mind of all this last June while sitting on a bench on London's Hampstead Heath. My bench, like many others, was almost entirely hidden; well off the path, delightfully overgrown, it sat at the top of a long-grassed meadow. It had a view. There was whimsy in its placement, and joy. It was thoroughly impractical. It had clearly been placed there to encourage one thing—solitary contemplation.

And sitting there, listening to the summer drone of the bees, I suddenly imagined George W. Bush on my bench. I can't tell you why this happened, or what in particular brought the image to my mind. Possibly it was the sheer incongruity of it that appealed to me, the turtle-on-a-lamppost illogic of it; earlier that summer, intrigued by images of Kafka's face on posters advertising the Prague Marathon, I'd entertained myself with pictures of Franz looking fit for the big race. In any case, my vision of Dubya sitting on a bench, reading a book on his lap—smiling or nodding in agreement, wetting a finger to turn a page—was so discordant, so absurd, that I realized I'd accidentally stumbled upon one of those visual oxymorons that, by its very dissonance, illuminates something essential.

What the picture of George W. Bush flushed into the open for me was the classically American and increasingly Republican cult of movement, of busy-ness; of doing, not thinking. One could imagine Kennedy reading on that bench on Hampstead Heath. Or Carter, maybe. Or even Clinton (though given the bucolic setting, one could also imagine him in other, more Dionysian scenarios). But Bush? Bush would be clearing brush. He'd be stomping it into submission with his pointy boots. He'd be making the world a better place.

Now, something about all that brush clearing had always bothered me. It wasn't the work itself, though I'd never fully understood where all that brush was being cleared from, or why, or how it was possible that there was any brush still left between Dallas and Austin. No, it was the frenetic, antithinking element of it I disliked. This wasn't simply outdoor work, which I had done my share of and knew well. This was brush clearing as a statement, a gesture of impatience. It captured the man, his disdain for the inner life, for the virtues of slowness and contemplation. This was movement as an answer to all those equivocating intellectuals and Gallic pontificators who would rather talk than do, think than act. Who could always be counted on to complicate what was simple with long-winded discussions of complexity and consequences. Who were weak.

And then I had it, the thing I'd been trying to place, the thing that had always made me bristle whenever I saw our fidgety, unelected president in action. I recalled an Italian art movement called Futurism, which had flourished in the first decades of the twentieth century. Its practitioners had advocated a cult of restlessness, of speed, of dynamism; had rejected the past in all its forms; had glorified business and war and patriotism. They had also, at least in theory, supported the growth of fascism.

The link seemed tenuous at best, even facile. Was I seriously linking Bush—his shallowness, his bustle, his obvious suspicion of nuance—to the spirit of fascism? As much as I loathed the man, it made me uneasy. I'd always argued with people who applied the word carelessly. Having been called a fascist myself for suggesting that an ill-tempered rottweiler be put on a leash, I had no wish to align myself with those who had downgraded the word to a kind of generalized epithet, roughly synonymous with asshole, to be applied to whoever disagreed with them. I had too much respect for the real thing. And yet there was no getting around it: what I'd been picking up like a bad smell whenever I observed the Bush team in action was the faint but unmistakable whiff of fascism; a democratically diluted fascism, true, and masked by the perfume of down-home cookin', but fascism nonetheless.

Still, it was not until I'd returned to the States and had forced myself to wade through the reams of Futurist manifestos—a form that obviously spoke to their hearts—that the details of the connection began to come clear. The linkage had nothing to do with the Futurists' art, which was notable only for its sustained mediocrity, nor with their writing, which at times achieved an almost sublime level of badness. It had to do, rather, with their antlike energy, their busy-ness, their utter disdain for all the manifestations of the inner life, and with the way these traits seemed so organically linked in their thinking to aggression and war. "We intend to exalt aggressive action, a feverish insomnia," wrote Filippo Marinetti, perhaps the Futurists' most breathless spokesman. "We will glorify war—the world's only hygiene—militarism, patriotism, the destructive gesture of freedom-bringers. . . . We will destroy the museums, libraries, academies of every kind. . . . We will sing of great crowds excited by work."

I knew that song. And yet still, almost perversely, I resisted the recognition. It was too easy, somehow. Wasn't much of the Futurist rant ("Take up your pickaxes, your axes and hammers and wreck, wreck the venerable cities, pitilessly") simply a gesture of adolescent rebellion, a FUCK YOU scrawled on Dad's garage door? I had just about decided to scrap the whole thing when I came across Marinetti's later and more extended version of the Futurist creed. And this time the connection was impossible to deny.

In the piece, published in June 1913 (roughly six months after Anderson walked out of the paint factory), Marinetti explained that Futurism was about the "acceleration of life to today's swift pace." It was about the "dread of the old and the known . . . of quiet living." The new age, he wrote, would require the "negation of distances and nostalgic solitudes." It would be, instead, an age enamored of "the passion, art, and idealism of Business."

This shift from slowness to speed, from the solitary individual to the crowd excited by work, would in turn force other adjustments. The worship of speed and business would require a new patriotism, "a heroic idealization of the commercial, industrial, and artistic solidarity of a people"; it would require "a modification in the idea of war," in order to make it "the necessary and bloody test of a people's force."

As if this weren't enough, as if the parallel were not yet sufficiently clear, there was this: the new man, Marinetti wrote—and this deserves my italics—would communicate by *"brutally destroying the syntax of his speech. Punctuation and the right adjectives will mean nothing to him. He will despise subtleties and nuances of language."* All of his thinking, moreover, would be marked by a *"dread of slowness, pettiness, analysis, and detailed explanations. Love of speed, abbreviation, and the summary. 'Quick, give me the whole thing in two words!'"*

Short of telling us that he would have a ranch in Crawford, Texas, and be given to clearing brush, nothing Marinetti wrote could have made the resemblance clearer. From his notorious mangling of the English language to his well-documented impatience with detail and analysis to his chuckling disregard for human life (which enabled him to crack jokes about Karla Faye Tucker's execution as well as mug for the cameras minutes before announcing that the nation was going to war), Dubya was Marinetti's "New Man": impatient, almost pathologically unreflective, unburdened by the past. A man untroubled by the imagination, or by an awareness of human frailty. A leader wonderfully attuned (though one doubted he could ever articulate it) to "today's swift pace"; to the necessity of forging a new patriotism; to the idea of war as "the necessary and bloody test of a people's force"; to the all-conquering beauty of Business.

One Year Later

2002

All national stories favor myth over hard fact, just as, to some extent, all personal ones do; few nations, however, have succeeded in erasing the hard facts of history as successfully, as utterly, as we have. But the empire of facts will have its say. Although Octavio Paz may have been right when he suggested that Americans have always preferred to use reality rather than to know it, we may yet have that acquaintance forced upon us.

Reality, of course, was not a fit subject this past year; we were a nation in crisis and had little patience for such frippery. Those who harbored notions of introducing it into the national debate, therefore, wisely held back and let the mythmakers have their day. But that day has passed. The storm of grief and fury has begun to abate, the patriotic surge, like the popularity of Osama bin Laden toilet paper, to recede. It may be time.

The spirit of pain is archaeological: it strips away—whether by brush or by pick—the layers of wishful thinking accumulated during times of peace. It scours and flays. It is by nature atavistic. At its best (unless it cuts too deep, comes too close) it can reveal the essential self, buried under a thin soil of misperceptions.

It seems almost trite to say it: whatever else last September's events have done, they have forced on us—or will, eventually—a

revolution in seeing. It will take time to understand what we have
been shown; as of yet, the work of re-vision has hardly begun.
Still, a few facts seem to be taking shape. A few truths, even. The
first is that, despite the muzzy pap of the globalists, who never
tire of limning their vision of a borderless, friction-free world, we
remain strikingly—even shockingly—tribal. The second is that
the source of this tribal identity—the three-century-old myth of
American exceptionalism—is alive and well. And not just alive
and well but ruddy-cheeked and thriving. Quieted for a time by
prosperity, it has revived under stress.

The third, more troubling, has to do with what that prosperity—
that long, sweet slumber—has done to us, and by us I mean the
so-called baby-boom generation of which I am a part. Indulged
by history as perhaps no generation has ever been indulged, here-
tofore largely excused from attendance, we've responded to our
wake-up call with an odd and often unadmirable mix of jingoistic bluster and domestic capitulation. Sensing an opportunity,
the Christian soldiers of our administration have ducked behind
the banner of our righteousness and are marching as to war (a
real war, this time), Colin Powell flapping like a small, decorative
banner in the wind.

But let me be clear. I am not interested in anatomizing the current administration's modus operandi: its made-for-TV bellicosity,
its positively Reaganesque oversimplifications, its ever-increasing
arrogance. I'm a novelist, not a policy wonk. I'm less interested in
our unelected representatives' predictable willingness to capitalize
on our confusion than I am in the source of that confusion. Why?
Because I sense something there, something not visible perhaps to
those blinkered by empiricism (even the soft-shelled empiricism
of the social sciences), something so large and amorphous that the
radar of the pollsters cannot detect it—less a historical truth than
a broadly cultural, intuitive one. I believe, to put it plainly, that
last year's attack was so traumatic to us because it simultaneously

exposed and challenged the myth of our own uniqueness. A myth most visible, perhaps, in our age-old denial of death.

Consider it. Here in the New Canaan, in the land of perpetual beginnings and second chances, where identity could be sloughed and sloughed again and history was someone else's problem, death had never been welcome. Death was a foreigner—radical, disturbing, smelling of musty books and brimstone. We wanted no part of him.

And now death had come calling. That troubled brother, so long forgotten, so successfully erased, was standing on our porch in his steel-toed boots, grinning. He'd made it across the ocean, passed like a ghost through the gates of our chosen community. We had denied him his due and his graveyards, watered down his deeds, buried him with things. Yet here he was. He reminded us of something unpleasant. Egypt, perhaps.

This was not just a terrorist attack. This was an act of metaphysical trespass. Someone had some explaining to do.

One Nation, under God

Some years ago, at the University of California, San Diego, a young woman raised her hand in the middle of a seminar I was then teaching on the first century of Rome and the dawn of the Christian era. She seemed genuinely disturbed by something. "I know you're all going to think this is crazy," she said, "but I always thought Jesus was an American."

A lovely moment. What she had articulated, as succinctly as I had ever heard it articulated, was the spirit behind three and a half centuries of American history: America as an elect nation, the world-redeeming ark of Christ, chosen, above all the nations of the world, for a special dispensation. What she had expressed, with an almost poetic compaction, was what the cultural historian Sacvan Bercovitch had termed the core myth of

America. Had John Winthrop been sitting at the table with us that foggy day in La Jolla, he would have understood what she was saying, and approved of it. As would Harriet Beecher Stowe. And Ronald Reagan. And, apparently, Attorney General John Ashcroft.

Stowe herself had made it all admirably clear in 1854: "The whole world," she wrote, in words notable for their lack of originality, "has been looking towards America with hope, as a nation specially raised up by god to advance a cause of liberty and religion." Others, from Henry David Thoreau to the evangelists of the Third Great Awakening, expressed the idea geographically, blending sacred and secular history, superimposing the religious metaphor over the actual land: America was bounded to the north by Canada, to the south by Mexico, to the East by Eden, and to the West by the Millennium. History moved from east to west. We had escaped fallen Egypt, crossed the sea, reinvented ourselves in the New World wilderness. Chosen for a special covenant with God, we would be "as a City upon a hill," to recall both John Winthrop's sermon aboard the *Arabella* in 1630 and Ronald Reagan's inaugural address from 1981. Inevitably, it was understood (is still understood), the westward-tending tides of Manifest Destiny would carry us on till the ship of state ground ashore on the pebbles of paradise.*

I had occasion to recall all this more than once last fall. I remembered it when I read that the sales of millennial tracts across the

---

* Is all this talk of covenants and destiny merely a vestigial limb, a speechwriter's rhetorical trope? Hardly. To understand the power of the myth in America today, we need only recall the recent reaction to the attempt by those godless liberals in the U.S. Court of Appeals to deprive us of our divine patrimony by excising the words "under God" from the Pledge of Allegiance.

nation were going through the roof because, according to biblical prophecy, the last days were to be preceded by great sorrow (as though only our sorrow would weigh in the record), when educated friends explained to me, with a kind of tragic gusto, that their entire worldview had been convulsed by the tragedy (and implied that it was vaguely un-American of me that mine had not), when a minister acquaintance confessed to undergoing a crisis of faith so severe that he was considering leaving the church.

When I wondered aloud to another acquaintance how it was possible for a man's faith to sail over Auschwitz, say, only to founder on the World Trade Center, I found myself quickly taken to task for both my myopia and my callousness—the product, he implied, of my excessively European sensibility. He himself had been in a state of crisis for two months. He slept badly, struggled with depression. His children were afraid to get in the subway or walk past a tall building, and there was nothing he could tell them. He was considering leaving New York and moving to Mexico. "How can you not see that everything is different now?" he concluded. "And anyway, who are you to decide when it's right for someone to have a crisis of faith?"

The answer to the second question was easy enough: no one, though I did reserve the right to wonder at the minister's timing, or where his faith might have been hiding when half a million human beings were being massacred in Rwanda, not a few of them in churches. But the first had me stumped. Simply put, I did not believe that everything was different now, particularly not in the ontological sense in which my friend intended it. Nor did I understand his apparent eagerness to proclaim it so.

Everywhere I turned that eerily cloudless, almost crystalline September, I encountered a similar dissonance. A few days after the attack, for example, Auden's "September 1, 1939" had blossomed in the vast, virtual fields of the Web:

Faces along the bar
Cling to their average day:
The lights must never go out,
The music must always play,
All the conventions conspire
To make this fort assume
The furniture of home;
Lest we should see where we are,
Lost in a haunted wood,
Children afraid of the night
Who have never been happy or good.

Even on the most superficial level, Auden's poem struck me as uniquely unsuited to the times. Rather than clinging to our average day, we seemed to be fairly trampling one another in our haste to assert that nothing would ever be average again, that the lights had indeed gone out and our homes become a haunted wood. Art? Music? Please. Colleagues in the School of the Arts at Columbia, where I teach (few writers, interestingly enough), seemed prepared to duel for the opportunity to testify to the Frivolity of Art in Times Like These. "It all feels so absurd," one said to me, referring to his own work. "What's the point?"

To which I couldn't answer, any more than I could have answered if he had been arguing the redundancy of beauty, or breathing. What could I say? That in June 1945, workers reclaiming the Reich's prisons in Moravia had found poems, folded into thick squares, stuffed up into the electrical wiring? Or that it seemed curious to me that a person locked in a cell, awaiting interrogation or death, would choose to write a poem on a piece of toilet paper, while another, arguably as safe as any human being has *ever* been in this world, would come to see art as a kind of decorative garnish, a sprig of parsley on the cultural plate? Should I have pointed out, perhaps, that art had always been an act of affirmation and resistance that, by its very complexity, worked against the shameful reductivism of fear, or that to believe otherwise was a luxury only the truly swaddled could afford? No, this seemed too obvious. Something else was at work here. I didn't understand it.

I understood it no more than I understood the poster that had appeared in a store on my corner the week of the attack bearing the slogan "Never, never, never, never give up!" "Give up what?" I wanted to ask the sober crowds on Broadway. "To whom?" A horrible thing had occurred, certainly. And those directly affected by the tragedy, like all victims of unspeakable things (like the mother of the teenager killed in a traffic accident the afternoon of the eleventh), deserved all of our compassion. But this was not London during the Blitz. Or Stalingrad in the winter of 1943. Or Sarajevo in 1994. Thousands of innocent people had died, true. But innocents had been dying for a while now—millions of them, mostly children, as quietly as melting snow each and every year. Surely we didn't think that just because . . .

Ah, but we did. How else to explain it? In our national heart of hearts, just below the global crust (with its multi- and poly- and inter- prefixcs), the conviction that we were different, apart, a City upon a hill, remained untouched. Why was this *"the biggest news event in the history of the world"* (my own, stunned italics), as the administration of New York's prestigious Stuyvesant High School told its students? Simple. Because it had happened here. To us. And, lest we forget, we Americans had been commissioned by God himself to bear the light of liberty and religion through-out all the earth. Rwanda? Bosnia? Couldn't help but feel sorry for those folks, but let's face it: Rwanda did not have a covenant with God. And Jesus was not a Sarajevan.

Hardly anyone outside the tattered fringe of the religious far right would have articulated it so bluntly, of course. And yet the fact remained: although the specifically Christian foundation of American exceptionalism had been largely buried by the years, the self-conception built upon it—however secularized and given over to mammon—remained intact. Our tragedy had exposed it, laid it bare, and torn it badly. Now I understood how we had managed to endure the slow disintegration of Bosnia with such fortitude: we had simply filed it, along with the events in Rwanda and Chechnya and Sierra Leone, under the rubric "Bad Things That Happen to People Who Are Not Americans." We seemed, on the whole, capable of bearing untold amounts of other people's pain and very little of our own. My brother-in-law's jokes about the famine in Ethiopia had been making the rounds before the dying there was even properly under way; by the summer of 2002, he had not told me a single World Trade Center joke. Humor, I realized, clearly had its limits—or borders, more precisely. The tribe still came first.

So much for globalism. What bothered me, however, was not so much the bald fact of our tribalism (which I found natural and excusable) as the hypocrisy with which we had denied it. What troubled me, specifically, was the kind of Benetton tokenism that allowed us to parade our global sympathies because we had eaten in a Sudanese restaurant last week, or featured a woman from Senegal in one of our ads. If we were going to weep for the victims of the attack on the World Trade Center and not for the dead of Srebrenica, it seemed to me, then we should have the courage to admit where the frontiers of our allegiance lay.

How close did tragedy have to come for us to bleed? Did we have to smell the smoke to have our imagination and our compassion activated? Did the victims have to be American? Or speak English? Was that enough? Or did they, perhaps, have to look like us as well? Was it possible, in other words, that our reaction to the tragedy was not wholly about those who had died—whom 99.9 percent of us had never known anyway—but about us? That what moved us, what woke us up to the fact that people had died—unexpectedly and tragically—was the uncomfortable thought that we might? It was a bit of a shock. Here in America, under the protective eye of Jesus, we could die. Now *that* was worth a crisis of faith.

Let me be as clear as possible here; I have no wish to be misunderstood. I believe that in this hyperbole-driven age, when the word *heroism* has been devalued to the point that men are deemed worthy of it simply for not abandoning their families, or for effectively smacking a leather ball with a stick, September 11 showed us not one but multiple examples of the real thing, unadulterated and potent and pure. In the last few moments, as the terrified crowds were streaming down the stairwells of the World Trade Center, men were running up, determined, in their minutes of allotted time, to save as many as possible. Ordinary human beings risked their lives (and, more than this, the unspeakable pain of those who loved them) to help others. This cannot be reduced, or contextualized. It can only be acknowledged, humbly, and perhaps with some bit of pride that this too our species is capable of.

This I believe. I believe as well, however, that a legitimate distinction can be made between those who, in one way or another, were directly touched by the tragedy and those who, like myself, were not. Who were never in any real danger. Who never missed a meal. The former are exempt from criticism. The latter are not. The former deserve either our reverence or our compassion. The rest of us merit neither, automatically. Courage, in general, is directly proportional to actual risk. Those who rushed in just after the buildings folded like great slabs of cake into the Manhattan pavement were the ones we heard from least. Those a hundred blocks north, meanwhile, cushioned even from the smell of the smoke by the grace of prevailing winds, scurried about, eager to bear witness to the suffering.

Their own, mostly. It didn't take long, alas, to note the disconcerting prevalence of the first person in these litanies: "I've been horribly traumatized. I'm terribly upset." A woman interviewed by the *New York Times* explained how she trembled every time she walked into a tall building, which could make for a lot of trembling in Manhattan. Others seemed to have found themselves, overnight, in a Samuel Beckett play: "A city block. A tree. Nothing to be done." They were thinking of moving out of the city, or maybe the country. And the three thousand souls still buried in the rubble just five miles south? Or the rescue workers, staggering with fatigue, trying to dig them out? Oh. Right. Them.

The solipsism in all this, the eagerness with which some individuals appropriated the tragedy for themselves, fascinated me. I'd seen its like before, though writ small. Among the pack I'd run with as a boy—a motley mix of runny-nosed urchins from Irish and Italian and Anglo-American families—there had been a big, soft kid I'll call Tommy Kelly. Outwardly no different from the rest of us, Tommy had a quirk we never tired of exploiting. When the pack turned inward—as it invariably would, less out of malice than sheer boredom—and began to pelt him with snowballs, he would not react as the rest of us did. He would not hunker down behind someone's mailbox and take his hits, knowing that soon enough it would be someone else's turn to draw the short straw. No, he would, in his own, entirely predictable way, fall apart. First he would select the smallest, scrawniest tagalong in the group and accuse him of starting it. Working himself into a froth, he would thrash this one unfortunate for a time, hoping thereby to draw the fire away from himself. When this didn't work (we knew what we were about, after all), he would eventually begin to pummel himself. Eagerly. Outdoing what was required. Picking up blocks of snow and ice, he would gleefully crack them over his own head; scooping handfuls of gritty slush, he would mash them in his own face. Sometimes he even managed to hurt himself, and ran home crying.

It took the Tommy Kellys of September 11 exactly three days

to find a scapegoat. A well-educated, appropriately liberal friend called with some "disturbing news." "They" were leaving, he said, abandoning the country in droves. JFK was packed. But that was not the real news. He had it "on good authority," from a friend connected to the New Jersey Department of Education, that "they" had kept their children out of school on the morning of September 11. Hard to believe? Sure. But records don't lie. And a nearly 100 percent absence rate allowed for only one conclusion: They had known. All of them.

I'm ashamed to say that, taken by surprise, and momentarily hamstrung by our friendship (this was a decent man I was talking to), I said little at the time beyond a few general expressions of disbelief, and thereby contributed, in some small way, to the proliferation of that idiocy. As is so often the case, I thought of a great many things to say after I'd hung up the phone. How, I might have asked (overlooking the patent absurdity of the entire accusation for a moment), were Muslim children identified on the school rosters in New Jersey? And were the political sympathies of their parents evident from their surnames? And why, if they were all in on the plot, and knew, therefore, that the planes would hit lower Manhattan, did they keep their children out of schools in New Jersey, for God's sake? And what of the wives and husbands and children of the Muslims who had died in the attack? And wasn't it a miracle on the order of the loaves and the fishes that this plot, so tightly controlled that it had slipped past the porous but still formidable radar of the information-gathering services of the United States government, had been common knowledge among twenty or thirty or fifty thousand Muslims, none of whom had let slip a word until the deed was done and they were getting into the cab, bound for JFK?

To our considerable credit, this brand of clumsy scapegoating (which might easily have gained in strength and virulence in a less heterogeneous society) quickly died. Which should have been the end of it. It wasn't. Lacking a convenient coven of witches to burn, disoriented by the fluttering of American flags, we simply jumped two steps up the conjugation and transferred the locus of our suffering from "them" to "us." We began to pummel ourselves. Life as we had known it was now effectively over, we declared. Nothing would ever be the same again. The ship of state was taking water. Best, therefore, to throw a few civil liberties overboard. Captain Ashcroft said so.

This eagerness to punish ourselves, to drag ourselves about in an ecstasy of suffering, would have been more explicable, more typically American, had it been coupled with some redeeming notion of our own sin. Throughout much of our history, after all, when hard times had hit, we had turned inward, assuming that the fault was ours and that we were being punished. Castigating ourselves for our shortcomings, we would flog ourselves into righteousness, thereby renewing our covenant with God and, by extension, the promise of America.

But this was something different. We felt as pure as the lamb. We had been struck for no reason. How could God do this to us? The result was a cultural mutation—a half jeremiad. Self-flagellation without self-scrutiny. Suffering without the need or capacity for atonement. We still flogged ourselves (we had that part down) but without quite knowing why.*

---

* Robert J. Tamasy, writing in *USA Today* after the recent furor over the Pledge of Allegiance, was the exception. Noting that "our nation is hurting deeply . . . in the aftermath of September 11th," he went on, like any minister in the Massachusetts Bay Colony, to assume that we had somehow been backsliding as a nation, and therefore should seek atonement for our sins. "Instead of seeking ways of removing God from everyday discourse," he wrote, "it might be better to consider the admonition of 2 Chronicles 7:14, 'If my people, who are called by my name, will humble themselves and pray and seek my face and turn from their wicked ways, then will I hear from heaven and will forgive their sin and heal their land.'"

Which is not to suggest that the old rituals had lost their power, only their ability to make us uncomfortable by suggesting that we were somehow complicit in our fate. Although shorn of its reflexive element (any mention of our own role in this was, quite simply, verboten), the jeremiad's power as a form of jingoistic exhortation and national renewal remained undiminished. Just as earlier crises—from colonial famine to the Civil War—had been quickly folded into the rhetoric of America's mission, so in 2001. The enfolding, of course, was slightly different now. Less than forty-eight hours after the attack, commemorative T-shirts and postcards were already for sale on Spring Street. From WTC chocolate bars to personal alarm systems ("Because, in trying times like these, one can't be too careful") to Estée Lauder's "America the Beautiful" compacts (with Austrian crystals for stars), the marketplace did its work: blurring the edges, dulling the pain, melding everything into the familiar lingo of dollars and cents. We felt better. History was once again back on the reservation. America was open for business. Evil would be punished, as our commander in chief assured us, though we would have to sign a very large check, and do exactly as he said, to make it so. The paradise of shoppers had replaced the other one as the telos of the American experiment, but the ability of the myth to regenerate itself, to seamlessly cover over any event, remained eerily intact.

Back to Egypt

A slightly narrower aperture. In August of 2001, my family and I, like tens of thousands of fellow Americans, traveled to Europe. The fresh green breast of the New World (a bit of a stretch for Jamaica Bay, but let it go) fell away below us, and eight hours and two movies later the clouds opened out on the half-harrowed fields and slate-roofed villages surrounding Prague. I had spent a good part of the journey staring at the global-positioning screens overhead, watching them calculate and recalculate precisely how far we had traveled and how much farther we still had to go. Would that it were that easy.

I spent the month that followed tripping over history, dogged by death. A personal thing, I suppose. My mother and, later, my father had chosen to return home after their forty-year sojourn in the New World. Czech had been my first language, Queens a suburb of Brno. In my head, I carried a wonderfully muddled version of Plutarch's *Parallel Lives*—Czech rather than Greek, American rather than Roman, but parallel all the same: on the one hand, Tomáš Masaryk, fleeing into exile; on the other, George Washington, already somehow triumphant, crossing the Delaware. On this side, Edvard Beneš, betrayed at Munich; on the other, Franklin, reeling in the thunderbolt on a key. All seemed to reinforce a series of binary oppositions, neat as the base pairs on a double helix: tradition versus self-determination; the humility born of experience versus the flushed triumphalism of power; the profound, almost filial attachment to place (the x coordinate to history's y) versus the freedom of the open road. Tragedy versus optimism. Death versus life.

I spent a good part of our vacation fighting against that inevitable sense of constriction, that horrible thickening of the atmosphere, that is the Old World's answer to the thin, boundless air of the West. Here they were again: the ubiquitous monuments, the unnumbered dead. Here were the generations from Adam down, staggering under the piled weight of the centuries. As I was—bearing history like an anvil. It hardly helped that my struggle itself was absurd, based on a cliché of continental identity more appropriate to Henry James's world than my own. I was indulging in a kind of double generalization, I told myself, ignoring not only the determined vapidity, the at times unbearable lightness of the new Europe, but also the historical shadows we Americans had grown since Nathaniel Hawthorne had argued we had none.

Still, for all that, a generalization to be reckoned with, difficult to deny.

What was I supposed to do with this knowledge, these layers of grief, like strata in stone, this constant folding-in of death? In every village a graveyard, dense with color; in every graveyard, tending their dead as if they were kohlrabi or turnips, the generations of the living: snipping, pruning, tossing the dead blooms into the tilting wooden wagon by the gate. It was to escape this infernal fussing, this easy familiarity with death—the three-year-old running down the path to bring her mother a trowel—that I'd gone west, to California, where no one seemed to die at all. Where once, while hunting bugs with my daughter in an overgrown field just outside the high desert town of Lone Pine, I had stumbled over a fallen gravestone and realized I was standing in the middle of a vast cemetery that no one, but no one, knew was there. That had been erased from the memory of men as surely as the wind had erased the lettering on its tablets. "You must understand," my mother had told me throughout my childhood, praising the communal business of caring for the dead (hoping, I suppose, to inoculate me against my culture's lack of respect for doneness, for gravity, or rather its inevitable issue, the grave), "the less you know of death, the more it frightens you."

But I had been born in America. We made history here; we didn't need to know it. To get away from all that depressing tonnage (which even then threatened to become my legacy), I did what Americans have always done: I ran. I moved as far west as I could without coming around again, stopping, finally, so close to the edge of the continent—the very lip edge of the millennium—that, from my door, a well-kicked soccer ball would have landed in the Pacific.

And yet here I was, a mere decade later, strangely famished yet not quite sure what it was, precisely, that I craved, what nourishment I hoped to derive from the experience. After all, what did all this have to do with me?

On a ramble through the forests of Moravia, three days before we left, we found ourselves eating our *rohlíky* and cheese in a walled country churchyard next to a nondescript white-plastered building topped by a wrought-iron skull. "That? That's the *kostnice*," said the pimpled young man in soccer shorts, desultorily scratching at the grass with a rake. The charnel house. He agreed, grudgingly, to let us in. We stepped inside. Our eyes adjusted to the gloom. Behind a small, gaudy altar to the Virgin were two columns so massive that for a moment I didn't understand what I was seeing: not stone, or mortar, but thousands of human shin bones, stacked lovingly each to each, forming ledges, pediments, smooth and cool as marble. Perhaps ten feet in diameter, topped by a delicate frieze of crania, the columns towered over us. For decoration, at regular intervals in the curving wall of bone, a skull had been lovingly set inside a human pelvis. Someone's mother. Someone's son. Like a bud at the center of a wide, white rose.

"V Jičíně jsou lepší"—there are better ones in Jičín—said the youth, impatiently shuffling his feet. I had no doubt it was true.

We returned home on September 4, walked out into the humid air and familiar lingo of New York. A week later, the Old World, so to speak, came to us. The *kostnice* was here now.

In the months that followed, we erased it, carted it off in trucks. It had nothing to do with us. There was nothing to learn. We were still innocent, apart.

Separateness from the world, for individuals as for nations, comes at a price, and it matters little if the isolation is physical or metaphysical. Our abiding sense of ourselves as a nation "under divine influence," as a recent letter to the *New York Times* put it, has already cost us a great deal. Perhaps, therefore, if we are to thrive in this not yet American century, if we are to prove capable of the kind of self-scrutiny necessary for survival, we may need to consider a reversal of direction.

Perhaps what we need to do is leave the City upon a hill, walk out of Canaan. Return to Egypt, filthy with history. The crowds thicken as you walk east—the crowds of the living and the dead. The doors of the *kostnice* are open. Enter it. You know this place, these bones. They are yours. Admit it.

Democracy and Deference

On the Culture of Obedience in America

2008

As this is in many ways a personal essay, it seems fitting to begin in the confessional mode. I suffer—have always suffered, I believe—from what is euphemistically referred to as "a problem with authority," by which I mean less an inherent distrust of it, though there *is* that, than a nearly absolute lack of respect for it. Authority conferred by money, position, connections, fame, etc., means slightly less than nothing to me. Should it happen to arrive accompanied by some genuine talent or virtue, it will be this I acknowledge, not the authority. At bottom, I just don't *feel* it—you know, that subordinate feeling, that acolyte's awe in the presence of the known— "Ohmigod, it's Brad!"—that overwhelming desire, when one is introduced to the Boss, to roll over and show him one's nippled belly, and though I've learned to compensate for this handicap the way autistic individuals learn to function "normally" by memorizing the gestures appropriate to particular social situations, I have to be constantly vigilant lest I miss my cue and salaam too late, or not at all.

I blame my parents, which is trite but traditional. Refugees from doubly battered Czechoslovakia, and therefore trained to measure with micrometer accuracy the gap between political rhetoric and lived experience, they knew better, much better, than to take the pieties of a liberal democracy straight. Nonetheless, six years after stepping onto the troubled shore of Senator Joseph McCarthy's America they had a son and promptly began to fill his head with nonsense. In America, they taught me, wealth and title and station alone meant nothing; talent and hard work were all. In America, allegiance was automatically owed to no one; respect had to be earned. In America, the president worked for us, and knew it, and the house we allowed him to live in for a time—that great white outie of the republic—was known as the People's House.

Would that I had been suckled by wolves.

The damage this training did was considerable, particularly as I, when faced with the obvious truth that only fools spoke their mind and the boss was always right, chose, perversely, to remain loyal to the lie—or the dream, if you like—thereby instantly cutting myself off from most avenues of advancement in America. Cemented into a posture of outraged denial, like the child who continues to believe in Santa Claus even after he's seen his father's wristwatch beneath the cotton-ball cuff, I became a writer, condemned to spend my days arguing for a vision, an antique notion of how things *should* be, in the face of a warehouse of evidence suggesting that the democratic spirit in America is a sentimental crust, no more, and the once-proud democratic self a cog—hardly noticeable, machined to a high level of tolerance—designed to catch and spin the gears of power.

Do I overstate my case? Perhaps. Once exposed, however, the deference factory's business, and its inevitable effects, are clearly visible. There's nothing particularly subtle about it; the construction of this New American, so wonderfully attuned to power, so heartbreakingly quick to heel or roll over (and bite those who don't), follows a three-step process—classroom to boardroom to political sphere—quite elegant in its simplicity. And make no mistake: though the process has no center—no coordinating cabal, no politburo—it clearly serves the interests of our new corporate ruling class, whose members, taking note, hurry ahead of the curling disk, frantically polishing and smoothing its course, assuring that all is friction-free.

Turn on the television to almost any program with an office in it, and you'll find a depressingly accurate representation of the "boss culture," a culture based on an a priori notion of—a devout *belief* in—inequality. The boss will scowl or humiliate you because he can; because he's the boss. And you'll keep your mouth shut and look contrite, even if you've done nothing wrong . . . because, well, he's the boss. Because he's above you. Because he makes more money than you. Because—admit it—he's *more* than you.

This is the paradigm—the relational model that shapes so much of our public life. Its primary components are intimidation and fear. It is essentially authoritarian. If not principally *about* the abuse of power,* it rests, nonetheless, on a generally accepted notion of power's privileges. Of its inherent rights. The Rights of Man? Please. The average man has the right to get rich so that he, too, can sit behind a desk wearing an absurd haircut, yelling "You're fired!" or pitch telephones at *domestiques,* or refuse to take any more questions; so that he too—when the great day comes—can pour boiling oil on the plebes clustered at the base of the castle

---

* The primary goal, after all, is not power per se, but a higher profit margin (achieved through a friction-free workplace), a motivation amply shared, in today's America, by those in the "business" of governing. I am assuming, of course, that there is still some useful distinction to be made between the public and the private sectors, between the Bush administration's CEOs and their brothers in industry, between the increasingly authoritarian behavior of our "elected" representatives and the generally authoritarian climate of the American workplace—which seems unlikely.

wall, each and every one of whom accepts his right to do so, and aspires to the honor.

You say I'm tilting at human nature? That the race of man loves a lord—and always has? That the democratic instincts of the so-called lower classes invariably dissipate as they rise in the world? That power (and what good is power if it can't be abused a little, no?) has always been one of the time-honored perks of success, and that, of all the lies told, the one about all men being created equal is the most patently absurd? Perhaps you're right. But surely one could argue that the American democratic experiment was at least in part an attempt to challenge this "reality," to establish a political and legal culture from which would emerge, organically, a new sensibility: independent, unburdened by the protocols of class, skeptical of inherited truths. Willing to be disobedient. To moon the lord.

Alas, if that was the plan, it went sideways a long time ago. In today's America, the majority is nothing if not impressed by power and fame (its legitimacy is irrelevant), nothing if not obedient. As for mooning the lord, the ass to the glass these days is more likely to be the lord's, and our own posture toward it, well, something short of heroic. Worse yet, should someone decide to take offense, and suggest that it is not the lord's place to act thusly, he will be set upon by the puckering multitude who will punish him for his impertinence.

At a White House reception a couple of years ago, President George W. Bush asked Senator-elect Jim Webb how things were going for his son, a marine serving in Iraq. "I'd like to get them out of Iraq, Mr. President," Webb replied. "I didn't ask you that," the president snapped back, according to a piece in the *New York Times*. "I asked you how your boy was doing."

Freeze the frame and pull back for a bit of context. Webb, a former secretary of the navy and a decorated Vietnam War veteran, had not only risked his own life in the service of his country but now had a child in harm's way, serving in an ill-conceived and criminally mismanaged war sold to the nation under false pretenses by the man standing in front of him. That other man— who over the course of his first forty years had shown no ability and little desire to distinguish himself in much of anything despite all the advantages that birth could offer—had sacrificed nothing. Called to serve in an earlier, equally ill-conceived and mismanaged war, he'd opted out of the principled stand (which would have required either saluting or protesting the war's injustice), cut the line to enter the National Guard, then declined to show up for attendance. In time, having winked and smirked his way to the presidency (a political miracle due, in no small part, to a bit of electoral sleight of hand and the timely aid of political hacks in the nation's highest court), he began his own war and people began dying at a fast clip.

Given all this, one might expect this second man to be nice. To show a modicum of respect. If a Lincolnesque moment of genuine reflection and anguish was a bit too much to ask, one might still have legitimately expected some small expression of sympathy, or—the slimmest paring of decency—a graceful evasion: "Maybe we can talk about this later, Jim." Should he still fall short, one could at least take comfort in the certainty that the American people would hold him accountable for his rudeness and presumption.

Which is precisely what many of them did—they held Jim Webb accountable. "I'm surprised and offended by Jim Webb," declared Stephen Hess, a professor at George Washington University, in a *New York Times* article titled "A Breach of Manners Sets a Tough Town Atwitter." Admitting that the president had perhaps been "a little snippy," Professor Hess went on to extol the democratic virtues of decorum and protocol, interrupting himself only long enough to recall a steel executive named Clarence Randall, who, having once addressed Harry S. Truman as "Mr. Truman" instead of "Mr. President," remained haunted by it for decades.

Hess wasn't the only one to be shocked by Webb's behavior. Letitia Baldridge, the "doyenne of Washington manners," termed the whole thing "a sad exchange." Judith Martin, a.k.a. Miss Manners, made the point that "even discussions of war and life and death did not justify suspending the rules," then declined to comment on *l'affaire* Webb-Bush, saying, "It would be rude of me to declare an individual rude."

But it was left to Kate Zernike, the author of the *Times* article, to place the cherry atop this shameful confection in the form of a seemingly offhand parenthetical: "(On criticizing the president in his own house, Ms. Baldridge quotes the French: *ça ne se fait pas*—'it is not done.'")

To which one might reply, in the parlance of my native town: Why the fuck not? *Répétez après moi:* It ain't the man's house. We're letting him borrow it for a time. And he should behave accordingly—that is, as one cognizant of the honor bestowed upon him—or risk being evicted by the people in favor of a more suitable tenant.

But let's not kid ourselves. The outrage over the Webb-Bush exchange was not really about decorum. Or manners. Or protocol. It was about daring to stand up to the boss. Rudeness? Stop. This is America. We're rude to each other more or less continually. We make mincemeat of each other on television, fiber-optically flame each other to a crisp, blog ourselves bloody. No, rudeness, as deplorable as it is, is not the point here, particularly as Webb, judged by any reasonable standard, wasn't remotely rude.

But wait—maybe rudeness is the point after all. Maybe rudeness, in our democratically challenged age, has morphed into a synonym for insubordination. If true, this explains a great deal. It suggests that in America today, only something done to those above us can qualify as rudeness. Done to those below it's something quite different—a right.

Which brings us to the case of former Secretary of State Colin Powell, whose dueling careers as soldier and statesman fought it out before the Security Council on that memorable day in March of 2003 as the nation prepared for war. The soldier, not surprisingly, dispatched the statesman, to our ongoing grief and Powell's everlasting shame.

We didn't know that at the time, of course. We trusted the man, though why, precisely, is hard to say. Was it his sonorous voice? His statesmanlike manner? His erect, soldierly carriage? Was it the fact that, unlike *his* bosses, he appeared to be a man of some substance, intelligence, and integrity? Whatever it was—and what does it say about us that we would base our trust on such airy ground?—he abused our faith in him. In a nutshell—or shell casing, perhaps—it came down to this: despite his doubts about the "intelligence" he had been provided, despite the fact that (as he himself admitted in his book, published long after any risk to his own career had passed) he spent days preparing for his pivotal speech by "trimming the garbage" from Vice President Cheney's "evidence" of Iraq's weapons programs and its ties to al Qaeda, Powell went ahead and shilled for the liars anyway. Why did he not threaten to expose the whole thing publicly? Because, as he has said, to do so would have betrayed the ethic of the loyal soldier he believed himself to be. Betraying the country—the nation as a whole as well as the thousands of front-line grunts from El Paso to Albany, never mind the tens of thousands likely to be caught in the cross fire—was judged the lesser offense.

What kind of culture defines "maturity" as the time when young men and women come to understand that adulthood means sacrificing principle to prudence, when they pledge allegiance to the boss—any boss—in the name of self-promotion and "realism"? What kind of culture defines adulthood as the moment when the self goes underground? One answer might be a military one. The problem is that while unthinking loyalty to one's commanding officer may be necessary in war,* it is disastrous outside it.

The notion of loyalty as inherently antidemocratic—indeed, the very mortar of the totalitarian state—is a tough idea to swallow, so let me be as precise as possible. On the personal or familial level, loyalty is not only generally admirable but in all likelihood evolutionarily hardwired into our genes. To the degree that it is institutionalized and mixed with power, however, it is toxic. Why? Because *loyalty*, all too often, is a buffered term for *obedience*, and *obedience* a euphemism for *cowardice*. Because loyalty qualifies individualism by discouraging the expression of individual opinion, recasting honesty as a type of betrayal and sacrificing individual responsibility to an easy expediency. Because, finally, loyalty to power, rather than to what one believes to be true, or right, can lead to the most horrendous abuses. Powell's excuse—that he did not want to betray the ethic of the loyal soldier—was precisely the one used by the defendants at Nuremberg, and if you say that the analogy is a reckless one, that Colin Powell is no Rudolf Hess but a generally decent man—an A student, a team player, a loyal employee, a good soldier—I'll agree, and say only this: God save us from men and women like him, for they will do almost anything in the name of "loyalty." And have. And will again.**

What we require most in America today, is seems to me, are bad soldiers: stubborn, independent-minded men and women, reluctant

---

* Though even here I hesitate, stalled by my lack of faith in the judgment of the general-bosses, in the purity of their motivations, as well as by the record of criminal incompetence and outright folly stretching from Gettysburg to Gallipoli and on, and on.

** It's only fair to add, however, that even though Powell's crime was dramatically smaller, so was the possible penalty for insubordination: not a bullet or a train ticket to Bergen-Belsen, but an endowed chair at the think tank or university of his choice.

to give orders and loath to receive them, loyal *not* to authority, nor to any specific company or team, but to the ideals of open debate, equality, honesty, and fairness.

Democracy, of course, is not an absolute but a relative value: "We're not perfect," the cry will sound, "but show us who is." I'll take a pass on perfection, but I'll say this: when it comes to the egalitarian attitudes democracy presupposes, the Brits, for all their wigged getups and parliamentary histrionics, have it all over us.

I think I realized this fully a few years back when I happened to see a BBC program featuring an "interview" with a member of the House of Lords who had voted in favor of supporting the U.S. invasion of Iraq. Though the member's name escapes me, I can still recall the breathtaking frankness of the "conversation," the utter lack of deference on the part of the interviewer, her willingness to insist on a satisfying answer and to mercilessly track down every attempt at evasion. So bare-knuckled was this exchange that I'm ashamed to say that my first reaction (this is how far I'd fallen) was discomfort. This was a major political figure, after all, and he was being treated like a truant with some explaining to do. More uncomfortable still, he himself seemed to accept that this grilling was the price one paid for public service, and that he'd better answer up and be quick about it.

My initial discomfort did not last long; by the time the man had been deemed sufficiently humiliated and sent packing, I was enchanted. It was as though I'd been permitted a glimpse of the world envisioned by the Founding Fathers, a world of educated, independent-minded citizens cognizant of the fact that theirs was the position of power, and, on the other side, representatives prepared to accept the fact that they were the hired help, laboring in a government—forgive me—of the people, by the people, for the people. And though the larger historical irony of the British showing us how to "do democracy" was not lost on me, I could not help but marvel, and envy, and wince at the unavoidable comparison.

But it's not just the formal, procedural differences between the two political cultures (the mandated brevity of the British election season, or the government's strictures on how much money a candidate can spend) that cast us in a sad and diminished light; it's the difference in spirit that lies behind, and informs, these distinctions.

In general, the Brits act as though the government is their business and they have every right to meddle in it. Americans, by and large, display no such self-assurance (unless they're throwing bricks at Washington, which underscores my point). To the contrary, we seem to believe, deep in our hearts, that the business of government is beyond our provenance. What accounts for this difference in attitude? My wife, whose family hails in part from England, has a theory: unlike us, the Brits don't confuse their royalty with their civil servants because they have both, clearly labeled. Acknowledging the apparently universal desire to defer, they channel that desire, wisely, into the place where it can do the least harm, a kind of political sump. Americans, on the other hand, lacking the royal catch basin, are squeezed between pretense and practice. Though we continue to pay lip service to the myth of the independent American, we understand it as a fiction—nice for a Friday night with a pint of Ben and Jerry's but about as relevant to today's world as a butter churn.

On the other side of the Atlantic, meanwhile, the Brits have become what we were once supposed to be. Consider the unavoidable (if largely symbolic) fact that our president lives ensconced in a palace, while 10 Downing Street is a row house. From there, consider the regal arrogance of the president and the president's men: their refusal to justify or explain policy, or abide by the constitution, or respond to the concerns of Congress. Next, consider the spectacle presented by the president's "meetings with the people," when he deigns to have them. Consider the extent to which he is scripted, buffered, coddled; the extent to which his audiences are screened to assure that they consist of cheerleaders whose "questions" are nothing more than praise couched in the shape of a question, or who don't even bother with the interrogative form and, like one woman at a Bush "rally," walk up to the microphone and say things like "My heroes have always been cowboys," then sit down to thunderous applause.

More? Recall an average press conference: President Bush striding to the podium, his slightly irritated, patronizing manner. Recall the press corps' sycophantic chuckling at every half-assed quip, its willingness to accept the most insulting answers, its downright Prufrockian ("and how should we presume") inability to challenge an obvious untruth. Consider the fundamental inequality implicit in the fact that the president is always addressed as "Mr. President," while septuagenarian journalists are invariably "Tom" or "Judy." Survey the whole, sad spectacle, soup to nuts, then dare to consider what the alternative might look like.

To indulge this fantasy, look up one of the question-and-answer programs on the BBC, and watch a prime minister sweat while answering questions from an audience specially selected, according to the *New York Times*, to assure that its members are "tough, and knowledgeable." Or take in one of the many lengthy press conferences, noting in particular how seriously the PMs take the process, or how, on being told that they haven't answered the question precisely, they apologize (apologize!) and try again. But why stop there? Make it hurt. Look up the session in which Prime Minister Tony Blair appears in front of a live audience whose indignant members demand an apology from him for going to war, and respond to his answers, as one woman did, with "That's rubbish, Tony."

Now recall that steel tycoon who, upon accidentally addressing the president as "Mr. Truman" rather than "Mr. President," was never able to forgive himself for the breach of etiquette. Which one is the citizen, and which the subject?

The real problem we face is not the Bush administration's imperial pretensions, its quasi-cultish stress on loyalty, or its instinctive suspicion of debate and dissent, but the extent to which the administration's modus operandi is representative of a society increasingly conversant with the protocols of subservience. In the long term, it is this tilt toward deference, this willingness to hold our tongues and sit on our principles, that truly threatens us, even more than the manifold abuses of this particular administration, because it makes them possible.

Over a century and a half after its publication, Tocqueville's *Democracy in America* has calcified into a reference work, a Bartlett's *Quotations* for journalists in a hurry. To those who still bother to read it, however, it offers something invaluable—a chance to plot our position on the road from, or to, despotism. Like any map, Tocqueville's doesn't presume to suggest where we will arrive, or when; it simply charts the terrain between two points—call them freedom and tyranny. Which direction we happen to be traveling, and how quickly, is up to us to determine, which "goal" we are currently approaching, the question at hand.

It's not a difficult question to answer. On the contrary, unless one has been in a deep sleep for the past seven years, the answer is glaringly obvious. Tyranny isn't something up ahead; it's right here. It's in the soil, in the very air we breathe. It's the *other* climate change, and no less real. The old tyranny, from which we emerged as a nation, has been transformed by the wonder-working ways of time and advertising into a powdered wig, a tricorn hat, and the God-given freedom to burn hot dogs; the new tyranny, meanwhile—infinitely more dangerous, Made in America—looms just ahead, so large as to be very nearly invisible.

Why haven't we noticed? Perhaps we're too busy, or histori-

cally ignorant, to recognize the political beast when it stands before us, slavering in the road. Perhaps we're so confused by the
rope-a-dope tactics of our would-be dictators—just look at them,
falling back into winking buffoonery one moment, attacking the
enemies of righteousness the next—that we don't quite know *what*
to think.

There's another possibility, of course—not a pretty one. Maybe
we're not out on the street protesting this administration's abuses
of power because we're no longer the people we once were, because we've been effectively bred for docility, trained to defer to
our leaders even though they reveal themselves, over and again,
to be dishonorable, incompetent men, even though they rob us
of what is rightfully ours, then present us with the bill for the
removal of our legacy.

Equality, Tocqueville pointed out, "insinuates deep into the
heart and mind of every man some vague notion and some instinctive inclination toward political freedom." But what about
inequality? Might it not, by precisely the same calculus, insinuate
"some instinctive inclination" toward political tyranny? Of course
it might. Once the idea of inequality is allowed to take root, a
veritable forest of ritualized gestures and phrases springs up to
reinforce it. The notion that some bow and others are bowed to
comes to seem natural; the cool touch of the floor against our fore-
head begins to feel right: from classroom to corporate cubicle to
the halls of Congress, deferential way leads on to deferential way,
and at the end of the road, as Tocqueville foresaw, stands a *baaa-
ing* polity "reduced to nothing better than a flock of timid and
industrious animals, of which the government is the shepherd."

Lincoln had it right: "If destruction be our lot we must ourselves be its author and finisher." We're off to a fine start.

Coda

A Quibble

2009

We have every reason to be pleased with ourselves. Bucking all recent precedent, we seem to have put a self-possessed, intelligent man in the White House who, if he manages to avoid being bronzed before his first hundred days are up, may actually succeed in correcting the course of empire. The bubble is rushing back to plumb; excitement is in the air. It would be churlish to quibble.

Still, let's. Although the guard at 1600 Pennsylvania Avenue has indisputably changed, although the new boss is *not* the same as the old boss, I'm less certain about us. I'd like to believe that we're a different people now; that we're more educated, more skeptical, more tough-minded than we were when we gave the outgoing gang of criminals enough votes to steal the presidential election, twice, but it's hard work; actual human beings keep getting in the way.

My neighbor, a high school teacher living about an hour outside New York City, wants to torture a terrorist. He's worried because he believes that Osama—excuse me, Obama—cares more about them than he does about us. He's never heard of the Spanish Inquisition. Another neighbor—an actual plumber, actually named Joe—wants Mark Haddon's *The Curious Incident of the Dog in the*

Night-Time tossed out of the high school library. Joe came by recently. Did I want my kids learning how to curse and kill dogs and commit adultery? he asked. I said that my kids already knew how to curse, and that I hadn't realized that killing dogs and committing adultery was something you had to learn. He showed me the book. He and his wife had gone through it with a blue highlighter and highlighted the words *crap, shit* and *damn* every time they appeared, on every page. They'd written to Laura Bush about it, and received a supportive letter in return, signed by the first lady. "You're a teacher," he said. "Don't tell me you support this kind of filth." I asked him if he'd read it. Well, no, he said, but he knew what it was about. He didn't really go in for reading, himself, he said.

I like a party as much as the next man, and I still have moments when I realize that the bastards are really, truly out and think that maybe, this time, it really is morning in America, but a voice from outside the ether cone keeps whispering that *we* haven't changed at all, that we're as dangerous to ourselves as we've ever been and that the relative closeness of the popular vote in this last election (given the almost embarrassing superiority of the winning ticket and the parade of catastrophes visited on the nation by the outgoing party) proves it. Go ahead and bask, this voice says, but that rumble you hear above the drums and the partymakers is real, and it's coming our way.

What we need to talk about, what *someone* needs to talk about, particularly now, is our ever-deepening ignorance (of politics, of foreign languages, of history, of science, of current affairs, of pretty much everything) and not just our ignorance but our complacency in the face of it, our growing fondness for it. A generation ago the proof of our foolishness, held up to our faces, might still have elicited some redeeming twinge of shame—no longer. Today, across vast swaths of the republic, it amuses and comforts us. We're deeply loyal to it. Ignorance gives us a sense of community; it confers citizenship; our representatives either share it or bow down to it or risk our wrath.

Seen from a sufficient distance (a decade abroad, for example), or viewed through a protective filter, like film, or alcohol, there can be something almost endearing about it. It can appear quaint, part of our foolish-but-authentic, naive-yet-sincere, rough-hewn spirit. Up close and personal, unromanticized and unfiltered, it's another thing entirely. In the flesh, barking from the electronic pulpit or braying back from the audience, our ignorance can be sobering. We don't know. Or much care. Or care to know.

What *do* we care about? We care about auto racing, and Jessica. We care about food, oh yes, please, very much. And money. (Did you catch the last episode of *I Love Money?*) We care about Jesus, though we're a bit vague on his teachings. And America. We care about America. And the flag. And the troops, though we're untroubled by the fact that the Bush administration lied us into the conflict, then spent years figuring out that armor in war might be a good idea. Did I mention money?*

Here's the mirror—look and wince. One out of every four of us believes we've been reincarnated; 44 percent of us believe in ghosts; 71 percent in angels. Forty percent of us believe God created all things in their present form sometime during the last 10,000 years. Nearly the same number—not coincidentally, perhaps—are functionally illiterate. Twenty percent think the sun might revolve around the earth. When one of us writes a book explaining that our offspring are bored and disruptive in class

---

* Ignorance, not to put too fine a point on it, is good for business, whether your particular business happens to be selling Prada handbags or presidents. It makes it so much easier to manufacture and manipulate those communities of habit and desire, those homogeneous blocks of consumers—sorry, citizens—who chant or vote on cue. "Drill, baby, drill."

because they have an indigo "vibrational aura," which means that they are a gifted race sent to this planet to change our consciousness with the help of guides from a higher world, half a million of us rush to the bookstores to lay our money down.

Wherever it may have resided before, the brain in America has migrated to the region of the belt—not below it, which might at least be diverting, but only as far at the gut—where it has come to a stop. The gut tells us things. It tells us what's right and what's wrong, whom to hate and what to believe and who to vote for. Increasingly, it's where American politics is done. All we have to do is listen to it and the answer appears in the little window of the eight ball: "Don't trust him. Don't know. Undecided. Just because, that's why." We know because we *feel*, as if truth were a matter of personal taste, or something to be divined in the human heart, like love.

I was raised to be ashamed of my ignorance, and to try to do something about it if at all possible. I carry that burden to this day, and have successfully passed it on to my children. I don't believe I have the right to an opinion about something I know nothing about—constitutional law, for example, or sailing—a notion that puts me sadly out of step with a growing majority of my fellow citizens, many of whom may be unable to tell you anything at all about Islam, say, or socialism, or climate change, except that they hate it, are against it, don't believe in it. Worse still (or more amusing, depending on the day) are those who *can* tell you, who know all about Islam, and then offer up a stew of New Age blather, right-wing rant, and bloggers' speculation that's so divorced from history and actual, demonstrable fact, that's *so* not true, as the kids would say, that the mind goes numb with wonder. "Way I see it is," a man in the Tulsa Motel 6 swimming pool told me last summer, "if English was good enough for Jesus Christ, it's good enough for us."

Quite possibly, this belief in our own opinion, regardless of the facts, may be what separates us from the nations of the world, what makes us unique in God's eyes. The average German or Czech, though possibly no less ignorant than his American counterpart, will probably consider the possibility that someone who has spent his life studying something may actually know more about it, or at least have an opinion worth considering. Not the American. Though perfectly willing to recognize expertise in basketball, for example, or refrigerator repair, when it comes to the realm of ideas, all folks (and their opinions) are suddenly equal. Thus evolution is a damned lie, global warming a liberal hoax, and Republicans care about people like *you*.

But there's more. Not only do we believe that opinion (our own) trumps expertise, we then go further and demand that expertise assume the position; demand, that is, that those with actual knowledge supplicate themselves to the Believers, who don't need to know *because* they believe. The logic here, if that's the term, seems to rest on the a priori conviction that belief and knowledge are separate and unequal. Belief is higher, nobler; it comes from the heart; it feels like truth. There's a kind of biblical grandeur to it, and as God's chosen, we have an inherent right to it. Knowledge, on the other hand, is impersonal, easily manipulated, inherently suspect. Like the facts it's based on, it's slippery, insubstantial— not solid like the things you believe.*

The corollary to the axiom that belief beats knowledge, of course, is that ordinary folks shouldn't value the latter too highly, and should be suspicious of those who do. Which may explain our inherent discomfort with argument. We may not know much,

---

* That an overwhelmingly Christian nation like the United States would have a belief-based polity should not surprise us, though it might well terrify us. In a country moved and swayed by the tides of faith, the separation of church and state is quaint, a legislative vestigial limb.

but at least we know what we believe. Tricky elitists, on the other hand, are always going on. Confusing things. We don't trust them. So what if Sarah Palin couldn't answer Charlie Gibson's sneaky question about the Bush Doctrine? We didn't know what it was, either.*

How did we come to this pass? We could blame the American education system, I suppose, which has been retooled over the past two generations to stamp out workers (badly), not skeptical, informed citizens. Or we could look to the "great wasteland" of television, whose homogenizing force and narcotizing effect have quite neatly corresponded to the rising tide of ignorance. Or we could spend some time analyzing the fungus of associations that has grown around the word *elitist*, which can now be applied to a teacher driving a thirteen-year-old Toyota, but not to a multi-millionaire CEO like Dick Cheney. Or, finally, we might look to the influence of the anti-elitist elites who, burdened by the weight of their Ph.D.s, will argue that the words *educated* and *ignorant* are just signifiers of class employed by the oligarchy to keep the underprivileged in their place, and then proceed to tell you how well Bobby is doing at Princeton.

But I'm less interested in the ingredients of this meal than in who's going to have to eat it, and when, and at what cost. There's no particular reason to believe, after all, that things will improve; that our ignorance and gullibility will miraculously abate; that the militant right and the entrenched left, both so given to cari-

---

* The notion that our elected officials should be our equals, or at least have the decency to hide it if they're not, must be one of the stranger offshoots of democratic liberalism. One suspects that, like most blooms, it is the result of stress. Suppressed everywhere it might have some practical or moral efficacy, egalitarianism in America has emerged in the bizarre notion that the congressman should be a regular guy, like me. This is equality we can believe in.

cature, will simultaneously emerge from their bunkers eager to embrace complexity; that our disdain for facts and our aversion to argument will reverse themselves. Precisely the opposite is likely. In fact, if we take the wider view, and compare today's political climate (the arrogance with which our leaders now conduct their extralegal adventures, the crudity of the propaganda used to manipulate us, our increasing willingness to cheer the lie and spit on the truth, just so long as the lie is ours) to that of even a generation ago, then extend the curve a decade or two into the future, it's easier to imagine a Balkanized nation split into rival camps cheered and sustained by their own propaganda than the republic of reason and truth so many of us want to believe in.

Traditions die hard, after all. Anti-intellectualism in America is a very old hat—a stovepipe at least, maybe even a coonskin. We wear it well; we're unlikely to give it up just like that. Consider, for example, what happens to a man or woman (today as ever) the minute they declare themselves candidates for office, how their language—their syntax, their level of diction, the field from which their analogies are drawn—takes a nosedive into the common pool. Notice how quickly the contractions creep in and the sleeves roll up. The analogy to high school seems appropriate; the pressure to adapt is considerable, and it's all in one direction—down. In American politics as in the cafeteria, the crowd sets the tone; it determines how to talk and what to think and who to like. It doesn't know much, and if you want in, you'd better not either. Should you want out, of course, all you have to do is inadvertently let on—for example, by using the word *inadvertently*—that you're a reasonably educated human being, and the deed is done.

Communicate intelligently in America and you're immediately suspect. As one voter from Alaska expressed it last fall, speaking of Obama, "He just seems snotty, and he looks weaselly." This isn't race talking; it's education. There's something sneaky about a man like Obama (or even John Kerry, who, though no Disraeli, could construct a sentence in English with a beginning, a middle, and an end) because he seems intelligent. It makes people uneasy. Who knows what he might be thinking?

But doesn't this past election, then, sound the all clear? Doesn't the fact that Obama didn't have to lower himself in order to win suggest that the ignorant are outnumbered? Can't we simply ignore the one-third of white evangelicals who believe the world will end in their lifetimes, or the millennialists who know that Obama's the Antichrist because the winning lottery number in Illinois was 666?

For starters, consider how easily things might have gone the other way had the political and economic climate not combined into a perfect political storm for the Republican Party; had the Dow been a thousand points higher in September, or gas a dollar cheaper. Truth is, we got lucky; the bullet grazed our skull.

Next, consider the numbers. Of the approximately 130 million Americans who voted this past November, very nearly half, seemingly stuck in political puberty, were untroubled by the possibility of Sarah Palin and the first dude inheriting the White House. At the same time, those of us on the winning side might want to do a cross-check before landing. How many of us—not just in the general election but in the primaries, when there was still a choice—voted for Obama because he was the *it* thing this season, because he was so likeable, because he had that wonderful voice, because he was black, because he made us feel as if Atticus Finch had come home? If nothing else, the fact that so many have convinced themselves that one man, thus far almost entirely untested, will slay the culture of corruption with one hand while pulling us out of the greatest mess we've known in a century with the other, suggests that a certain kind of "clap your hands if you believe" naïveté crosses the aisle at will.

But the electorate, whatever its issues, is not the real problem.

The real problem, the unacknowledged pit underlying American democracy, is the 38 percent of the population who didn't move, didn't vote. Think of it: a country the size of Germany—83 million people—within our own borders. Many of its citizens, after decades of watching the status quo perpetuate itself, are presumably too fed up to bother, a stance we can sympathize with and still condemn for its petulance and immaturity, its unwillingness to acknowledge the fact that in every election there is a better and a worse choice. Millions of others, however, are adults who don't know what the Bill of Rights is, who have never heard of Lenin, who think Africa is a nation, who have never read a book. I've talked to enough of them to know that many are decent people, and that decency is not enough. Witches are put to the stake by decent people. Ignorance trumps decency any day of the week.

Praise me for a patriot or warm up the pillory, it comes down to the unpleasant fact that a significant number of our fellow citizens are now as greedy and gullible as a boxful of puppies; they'll believe anything; they'll attack the empty glove; they'll follow that plastic bone right off the cliff. Nothing about this election has changed that fact. If they're ever activated—if the wrong individual gets to them, in other words, before the educational system does—we may live to experience a tyranny of the majority Tocqueville never imagined.

Dehumanized

On the Selling (Out) of American Education,
and What It Costs Us

2009

Knowledge of human nature is the
beginning and end of political education.
—HENRY ADAMS

Many years ago, my fiancée attempted to lend me a bit of respecta-
bility by introducing me to my would-be mother-in-law as a future
Ph.D. in literature. From Columbia, I added, polishing the apple
of my prospects. She wasn't buying it. "A doctor of philosophy," she
said. "What're you going to do, open a philosophy store?"

A spear is a spear—it doesn't have to be original. Unable to
come up with a quick response and unwilling to petition for a
change of venue, I ducked into low-grade irony. More like a stand,
I said. I was thinking of stocking Chaucer quotes for the holidays,
lines from Yeats for a buck fifty.

And that was that. I married the girl anyway. It's only now, re-
calling our exchange, that I can appreciate the significance—the
poetry, really—of our little pas de deux. What we unconsciously

acted out, in compressed, almost haikulike form *(A philosophy store? / I will have a stand / sell pieces of Auden at two bits a beat)* was the essential drama of American education today.

It's a play I've been following for some time now. It's about the increasing dominance—scratch that, the unqualified triumph—of a certain way of seeing, of reckoning value. It's about the victory of whatever can be quantified over everything that can't. It's about the quiet retooling of American education into an adjunct of business, an instrument of production.

The play's almost over. I don't think it's a comedy.

State of the Union

> *And then there's amortization,*
> > *the deadliest of all,*
> *Amortization*
> > *of the heart and soul.*
> —VLADIMIR MAYAKOVSKY

Despite the determinisms of the day, despite the code breakers, the wetware specialists, the patient unwinders of the barbed wire of our being, this I feel is true: that we are more nurture than nature; that what we are taught, generally speaking, is what we become; that torturers are made slowly, not minted in the womb. As are those who resist them. I believe that what rules us is less the material world of goods and services than the immaterial one of whims, assumptions, delusions, and lies; that only by studying this world can we hope to shape how it shapes us; that only by attempting to understand what used to be called, in a less embarrassed age, "the human condition" can we hope to make our condition more human, not less.

All of which puts me, and those in the humanities generally, at something of a disadvantage these days. In a high-speed corporate culture, hypnotized by quarterly results and profit margins, the gradual sifting of political sentiment is of no value; in a horizontal world of "information" readily convertible to product—the lowest, most reductive definition of utility—the verticality of wisdom has no place. Show me the spreadsheet on skepticism.

You have to admire the skill with which we've been out-maneuvered; there's something almost chesslike in the way other side has narrowed the field, neutralized lines of attack, co-opted the terms of battle. It's all about them now; every move we make plays into their hand, confirms their values. Like the narrator in Mayakovsky's "Conversation with a Tax Collector about Poetry," we're being forced to account for ourselves in the other's idiom, to argue for "the place of the poet / in the workers' ranks." It's not working.

What is taught, at any given time, in any culture, is an expression of what that culture considers important. That much seems undebatable. How "the culture" decides, precisely, on what matters, how openly the debate unfolds—who frames the terms, declares a winner, and signs the check—well, that's a different matter. Real debate can be short-circuited by orthodoxy, and whether that orthodoxy is enforced through the barrel of a gun or backed by the power of unexamined assumption, the effect is the same.

In our time, orthodoxy is economic. Money doesn't talk, it roars. Popular culture fetishizes it, our entertainments salaam to it (how many millions for sinking that putt, accepting that trade?), our artists are ranked by and revered for it.* There is no institution wholly

---

* To glance at the "Arts in the News" column of the *New York Times* is to understand that the only news that's fit to print is monetary: which record went platinum, which show garnered the highest ratings, which novel received the fattest advance, which painting sold at Sotheby's for how many millions. The revenue generated by our words and deeds isn't just part of the conversation, it *is* the conversation; market share is the new talent.

apart. Everything submits, everything must, sooner or later, pay fealty to the market; thus cost-benefit analyses on raising children, on cancer medications, on clean water, on the survival of species, including—in the last, last analysis—our own. If humanity has suffered under a more impoverishing delusion, I'm not aware of it.

That education policy should reflect the zeitgeist shouldn't surprise us; capitalism, after all, has a wonderful knack for marginalizing (or co-opting) systems of value that might pose an alternative to its own. Still, capitalism's success in this case is particularly elegant: by bringing education to heel, by forcing it to meet its criteria for "success," the market is well on the way to controlling a majority share of the one business that might offer a competing product, that might question its assumptions. It's a neat trick. The problem, of course, is that by its success (and make no mistake, it *is* succeeding), we are made vulnerable. By downsizing what is most dangerous (and most essential) about our education, namely, the deep civic function of the arts and the humanities, we're well on the way to producing a nation of employees, not citizens. Thus is the world made safe for commerce, but not safe.

We're pounding swords into cogs. They work in Pyongyang, too.

Capital Investment

This is exactly what life is about. You get a paycheck every two weeks. We're preparing children for life.
        —CHANCELLOR MICHELLE RHEE
        DISTRICT OF COLUMBIA SCHOOLS

The question is straightforward enough: what do we teach, and why? One might assume that in an aspiring democracy like ours the answer would be equally straightforward: we teach whatever contributes to the development of autonomous human beings; we teach, that is, in order to expand the census of knowledgeable, reasoning, independent-minded individuals both sufficiently familiar with the world outside themselves to lend their judgments compassion and breadth (and thereby contribute to the political life of the nation), and sufficiently skilled to find productive employment. In that order. Our primary function, in other words, is to teach people, not tasks; to participate in the complex and infinitely worthwhile labor of forming citizens, men and women capable of furthering what's best about us and forestalling what's worst. It is only secondarily—one might say incidentally—about producing workers.

I'm joking, of course. Education in America today is almost exclusively about the GDP. It's about investing in our human capital, and please note what's modifying what. It's about ensuring that the United States does not fall from its privileged perch in the global economy. And what of our privileged political perch, you ask, whether legitimate or no? Thank you for your question. Management has decided that the new business plan has no room for frivolity. Those who can justify their presence in accordance with its terms may remain; the rest will be downsized or discontinued. Alternatively, since studies have suggested that humanizing the workspace may increase efficiency, a few may be kept on, the curricular equivalent of potted plants.

If facetiousness is an expression of frustration, it does not necessarily follow that the picture it paints is false. The force of the new dispensation is stunning. Its language is the language of banking—literal, technocratic, wincingly bourgeois; its effects are visible, quite literally, everywhere you look.

Start with the newspaper of record. In a piece by *New York Times* editorialist Brent Staples, we learn that the American education system is failing "to produce the fluent writers required by the new economy." No doubt it is, but the sin of omission here is both telling and representative. Might there be another reason for seeking to develop fluent writers? Could clear writing have some relation to clear thinking, and thereby have, perhaps, some political efficacy? If so, neither Staples nor his readers, writing in to the *Times,* think to mention it. Writing is "a critical strategy that we can offer students to prepare them to succeed in the workplace." Writing skills are vital because they promote "clear, concise communications, which all business people want to read." "The return on a modest investment in writing is manifold," because "it strengthens competitiveness, increases efficiency and empowers employees." And so on, without exception. The chairman of the country's largest association of college writing professors agrees. The real problem, he explains, is the SAT writing exam, which "hardly resembles the kinds of writing people encounter in business or academic settings." An accountant, he argues, needs to write "about content related to the company and the work in which she's steeped." It's unlikely that she'll "need to drop everything to give the boss 25 minutes on the Peloponnesian War or her most meaningful quotation."

What's depressing here is that this is precisely the argument heard at parent-teacher meetings across the land: What good is it in the real world? When is the boss ever going to ask my Johnny about the Peloponnesian War? As if Johnny had agreed to have no existence outside his cubicle of choice. As if he wasn't going to be a husband, or a father (or listen to Rush, or Glenn Beck, while driving home from the office). As if he wasn't going to inherit, willy-nilly, the holy right of gun ownership and the power of the vote.

At times, the failure of decent, intelligent, reliably humane voices like Staples's to see the political forest for the economic trees is breathtaking. In a generally well-intentioned editorial, one of Staples's colleagues at the *Times,* Nicholas Kristof, argues that we can't "address poverty or grow the economy" unless we do something about the failure of our schools. So far, so good, though one might quibble that addressing poverty and growing the economy are not the same thing.

But never mind, because the real significance of the failure of our schools is soon made manifest. "Where will the workers come from," Kristof worries, "unless students reliably learn science and math?" If our students "only did as well as those in several Asian countries in math and science, our economy would grow 20 percent faster." The problem, though, is that while our school system was once the envy of all (a "first-rate education," we understand by this point, is one that grows the economy), now only our white suburban schools are "comparable to those in Singapore, which may have the best education system in the world."

Ah, Singapore. You'll hear a good deal about Singapore if you listen to the chorus of concern over American education. If only we could be more like Singapore. If only our education system could be as efficient as Singapore's. You say that Singapore might not be the best model to aspire to, that in certain respects it more closely resembles Winston Smith's world in *1984* than Thomas Jefferson's? What does that have to do with education?

And the beat goes on. Still another *Times* editorialist, Thomas Friedman, begins a piece on the desperate state of American education by quoting Bill Gates. Gates, Friedman informs us, gave a "remarkable speech" in which he declared that "American high schools are obsolete." This is bad, Friedman says. Bill Gates is telling us that our high schools, "even when they are working exactly as designed—cannot teach our kids what they need to know today."

What *do* our kids need to know today? As far as Friedman is concerned, the answer is obvious: whatever will get them hired by Bill Gates. "Let me translate Mr. Gates's words," he writes. What Mr. Gates is saying is: "If we don't fix American education, I will not be able to hire your kids." Really worried now, Friedman goes to talk to former Harvard president and head of the National

Economic Council, Lawrence Summers, who explains that "for the first time in our history," we're facing "competition from low-wage, high-human-capital communities, embedded within India, China, and Asia." The race is on. "In order to thrive," Summers says, we will "have to make sure that many more Americans can get as far ahead as their potential will take them," and quickly, because India and China are coming up on the inside. It's "not just about current capabilities," Friedman concludes, by this point quoting the authors of *The Only Sustainable Edge*, "it's about the relative pace and trajectories of capability-building."

Sustainable edges. Returns on capital investment. Trajectories of capability-building. What's interesting here is that everyone speaks the same language, everyone agrees on the meaning of the terms. There's a certain country club quality to it. We're all members. We understand one another. We understand that the capabilities we should be developing are the capabilities that will "get us ahead." We understand that Bill Gates is a logical person to talk to about education because billionaire capitalists generally know something about running a successful business, and American education is a business whose products (like General Motors', say), are substandard, while Singapore's are kicking ass. We understand that getting ahead of low-wage, high-human-capital communities will allow us "to thrive."

Unlike most country clubs, alas, this one is anything but exclusive; getting far enough beyond its gates to ask whether that last verb might have another meaning can be difficult. Success means success. To thrive means to thrive. The definitions of *investment, accountability, value, utility* are fixed and immutable; they are what they are. Once you've got that down, everything is easy: according to David Brooks (bringing up the back of my *Times* parade), all we need to do is make a modest investment in "delayed gratification skills." Young people who can delay gratification "can master the sort of self-control that leads to success"; they "can sit through sometimes boring classes" and "perform rote tasks." As a result, they tend to "get higher SAT scores," to gain acceptance to better colleges, and to have, "on average, better adult outcomes."*

A little of this can go a long way, and there's a lot of it to be had. When it comes to education in America, with very few exceptions, this is the conversation and these are its terms. From the local PTA meeting to the latest Presidential Commission on Education, the only subject under discussion, the only real criterion for investment—in short, the alpha and omega of educational policy—is jobs. Is it any wonder, then, that our educational priorities should be determined by business leaders, or that the relationship between industry and education should increasingly resemble the relationship between a company and its suppliers, or that the "suppliers" across the land, in order to make payroll, should seek to please management in any way possible, to demonstrate the viability of their product?

Consider the ritual of addressing our periodic "crises in education." The call to arms comes from the business community. We're losing our competitive edge, sounds the cry. Singapore is pulling ahead. The president swings into action. He orders up a blue chip commission made up of high-ranking business executives (the 2006 Commission on the Future of Higher Education

---

* There's something almost sublime about this level of foolishness. By giving his argument a measured, mathematical air (the students only achieve better adult outcomes "on average"), Brooks hopes that we will overlook both the fact that his constant (success) is a variable, and that his terms are way unequal, as the kids might say. One is reminded of the scene in the movie *Proof* in which the mathematician played by Anthony Hopkins, sliding into madness, begins a proof with "Let X equal the cold." Let higher SAT scores equal successful adult outcomes.

led by business executive Charles Miller, for example) to study the problem and come up with "real world" solutions.

Thus empowered, the commission crunches the numbers, notes the depths to which we've sunk, and emerges into the light to underscore the need for more accountability. To whom? Well, to business, naturally. To whom else would you account? And that's it, more or less. Cue the curtain. The commission's president answers all reasonable questions. Everyone goes home and gets with the program.

It can be touching to watch supporters of the arts contorting themselves to fit. In a brochure produced by the Education Commission of the States, titled "The Arts, Education and the Creative Economy," we learn that supporting the arts in our schools is a good idea because "state and local leaders are realizing that the arts and culture are vital to economic development." In fact, everyone is realizing it. Several states "have developed initiatives that address the connections between economic growth and the arts and culture." The New England states have formed "the Creative Economy Council . . . a partnership among business, government and cultural leaders."* It seems that "a new economy has emerged . . . driven by ideas, information technology and globalization" (by this point, the role of painting, say, is getting a bit murky), and that "for companies and organizations to remain competitive and cutting edge, they must attract and retain individuals who can think creatively."

You can almost see the air creeping back into the balloon: We can do this! We can make the case to management! We can explain, as Mike Huckabee does, that trimming back funding for the arts would be shortsighted because "experts and futurists warn that the future economy will be driven by the 'creative

---

* The ranking of "leaders" here is worth noting given the ostensible subject of the advertisement.

class.'" We can cite "numerous studies" that "affirm that a student schooled in music improves his or her SAT and ACT scores in math," and that "creative students are better problem solvers . . . a trait the business world begs for in its work force." They'll see we have some value after all. They'll let us stay.

To show that they, too, get it, that like Cool Hand Luke they've "got their mind right," our colleges and universities smile and sway with the rest. In "A Statement by Public Higher Education Leaders Convened by the Carnegie Corporation of New York"—to pick just one grain of sand from a sandbox of evidence—we learn that our institutions of higher learning are valuable because they can "help revitalize our nation's economy and educate and train the next generations to meet the challenges of global competition." Both the tune and the lyrics should be familiar by now. "The present economic crisis requires an investment in human capital." And where better to invest than in our colleges and universities, whose innovative researchers have "invented the technologies that have fueled economic progress and enhanced America's economic competitiveness"? The statement's undersigned, representing colleges and universities from California to New Hampshire, conclude with a declaration of faith: "Leaders of the country's public higher education sector are committed to create a long-term plan *to serve the nation by enhancing public universities' critical role in creating jobs*, increasing graduates, enhancing the quality and skills of the workforce, and assisting in national technology and energy initiatives through research."

Think of my italics above as a hand going up in the back of the audience. Could there exist, buried under our assumptions, another system of value, an alternate set of definitions? Could our colleges and universities—indeed, our entire education system— have another, truly "critical role," which they ignore at our peril? A role that might "serve the nation" as well?

The Case for the Humanities

Only the educated are free.
—EPICTETUS

Rain does not follow the plow. Political freedom, whatever the market evangelists may tell us, is not an automatic by-product of a growing economy; democratic institutions do not spring up, like flowers at the feet of the magi, in the tire tracks of commerce. They just don't. They're a different species. They require a different kind of tending.

The case for the humanities is not hard to make, though it can be difficult—to such an extent have we been marginalized, so long have we acceded to that marginalization—not to sound either defensive or naive. The humanities, done right, are the crucible in which our evolving notions of what it means to be fully human are put to the test; they teach us, incrementally, endlessly, not what to do, but how to be. Their method is confrontational, their domain unlimited, their "product" not truth but the reasoned search for truth, their "success" something very much like Frost's momentary stay against confusion.

They are thus, inescapably, political. Why? Because they complicate our vision, pull our most cherished notions out by the roots, flay our pieties. Because they grow uncertainty. Because they expand the reach of our understanding (and therefore our compassion), even as they force us to draw and redraw the borders of tolerance. Because out of all this work of self-building might emerge an individual capable of humility in the face of complexity; an individual formed through questioning and therefore unlikely to cede that right; an individual resistant to coercion, to manipulation and demagoguery in all their forms. The humanities, in short, are a superb delivery mechanism for what we might call democratic values. There is no better that I am aware of.

This, I would submit, is value—and cheap at the price. This is utility of a higher order. Considering where the rising arcs of our ignorance and our deference lead, what could represent a better investment? Given our fondness for slogans, our childlike susceptibility to bullying and rant, our impatience with both evidence and ambiguity, what could earn us, over time, a better rate of return?

Like a single species taking over an ecosystem, like an elephant on a seesaw, the problem today is disequilibrium. Why is every Crisis in American Education cast as an economic threat and never a civic one? In part, because we don't have the language for it. Our focus is on the GDP. On growth. On the usual economic indicators. There are no corresponding "civic indicators," no generally agreed upon warning signs of political vulnerability, even though the inability of more than two-thirds of our college graduates to read a text and draw rational inferences could be seen as the political equivalent of runaway inflation or soaring unemployment.

If we lack the language, and therefore the awareness, to right the imbalance between the vocational and the civic, if education in America—despite the heroic efforts of individual teachers— is no longer in the business of producing the kinds of citizens necessary to the survival of a democratic society, it's in large part because the time-honored civic function of our educational system has been ground up by the ideological mills of both the right and the left into a radioactive paste called values education and declared off limits. Consider the irony. Worried about indoctrination, we've short-circuited argument. Fearful of propaganda, we've taken away the only tools that could detect and counter it. "Values" are now the province of the home. And the church. How convenient for the man.

How does one "do" the humanities value-free? How does one

teach history, say, without grappling with what that long parade of genius and folly suggests to us? How does one teach literature other than as an invitation, a challenge, a gauntlet—a force fully capable of altering not only what we believe but also how we see? How does one teach rhetoric without awakening students to the manipulations of language and thereby inoculating them against the pap delivered by both the left and the right? The answer is, of course, that one doesn't. One teaches some toothless, formalized version of these things, careful not to upset anyone, despite the fact that upsetting people is arguably the very purpose of the arts and perhaps of the humanities in general.

Even a dessicated, values-free version of the humanities has the potential to be dangerous, though, if only because it is so difficult to say where the individual mind might wander off to while reading, what unsettling associations might suggest themselves, what unscripted, unapproved questions might float to the surface. It's been said before: in the margins of the page, over the course of time, for the simple reason that we shape every book we read and are slightly shaped by it in turn, we become who we are. Which is to say, individuals just distinct enough from one another in our orientation toward "the truth" or "the good" to be difficult to control.

This "deep civic" function of the humanities, not easily reducible to the politics of left or right but politically combustible nonetheless, is something understood very well by totalitarian societies, which tend to keep close tabs on them, and to circumscribe them in direct proportion to how stringently they control their own populations. This should neither surprise nor comfort us. Why would a repressive regime support a force superbly designed to resist it? Rein in the humanities effectively enough—whether through active repression, fiscal starvation, or linguistic marginalization—and you create a space, an opportunity. Dogma adores a vacuum.

Mathandscience

Nobody was ever sent to prison for
espousing the wrong value for the
Hubble constant.
—DENNIS OVERBYE

Nothing speaks more clearly to the relentlessly vocational bent in American education than its long-running affair with math and science. I say "affair" because I am kind; in truth the relationship is obsessive, exclusionary, altogether unhealthy. Whatever the question, math and science (so often are they spoken of in the same breath, they've begun to feel singular) are, or is, the answer. They make sense; they compute. They're everything we want: a solid return on capital investment, a proven route to "success." Everything else can go fish.

Do we detect a note of bitterness, a hint of jealousy? No doubt. There's something indecent about the way math and science gobble up market share. Not content with being heavily subsidized by both government and private industry as well as serving as a revenue-generating gold mine for higher education (which divides up the profits from any patents and passes on research expenses to students through tuition increases—effectively a kind of hidden "science tax"), math and science are now well on the way to becoming the default button of choice for anyone having trouble deciding where to park his (or the taxpayers') money, anyone trying to burnish his no-nonsense educational bona fides, or, most galling, anyone looking for a way to demonstrate his or her civic pride.

But let me be clear: I write this not to provide tinder to our inquisitors, ever eager to sacrifice the spirit of scientific inquiry in the name of some latter-day misapprehension. That said, I see no contradiction between my respect for science and my humanist's discomfort with its ever-greater role in American culture, its ever-burgeoning coffers, its often dramatically antidemocratic ways, its symbiotic relationship with government, with industry, with our increasingly corporate institutions of higher learning. Triply protected from criticism by the firewall of their jargon (which immediately excludes the nonspecialist and assures a jury of motivated and sympathetic peers), their economic efficacy, and the immunity conferred by conveniently associated terms like *progress* and *advancement,* the sciences march, largely untouched, under the banner of the inherently good.* And this troubles me.

It troubles me because there are many things "math and science" do well, and some they don't. And one of the things they don't do well is democracy. They have no aptitude for it, no connection to it, really. Which hasn't prevented some in the sciences from arguing precisely the opposite, from assuming even this last, most ill-fitting mantle.

In a giddy and cheerfully self-immolating essay in the *New York Times* titled "Elevating Science, Elevating Democracy," for example, Dennis Overbye opens with a paean to science as a "utopian anarchy" (at least, he adds, without a hint of a wink, "as utopian as any community largely dependent on government and corporate financing can be"), then claims, as if declaring the existence of gravity, that science is about democracy. In fact, "if we're not practicing good science," he states, "we probably aren't practicing good democracy." To cinch his case, he quotes Hu Yaobang, the Chinese Communist Party's general secretary, who in 1980 declared that science "opposes the beaten path and dares to destroy outmoded conventions and bad customs."

Having raised this wobbly tent, Overbye promptly drives a truck over it. Mr. Hu's inspiring words, he notes, have sadly "not yet

---

* Despite the "debates" surrounding issues like evolution, climate change, and stem cell research, science in the West continues to enjoy almost unimaginable fiscal and cultural advantages.

been allowed to come true in China" because Hu himself was purged. (Science, he neglects to add, has done quite well in China regardless.) So, could this be a problem? Could the case of Mr. Hu suggest that the trickle-over theory, which holds that science's spirit of questioning will automatically infect the rest of society, is, in fact, false? Could it be that science actually keeps to its reservation, which explains why scientists tend to get in trouble, generally speaking, only when they step outside the lab?* Though he's not aware of it, Overbye has already answered these questions in the affirmative. Science is a good thing "to get gooey about," he notes, because "nobody was ever sent to prison for espousing the wrong value for the Hubble constant."

Which is both true and precisely, even eloquently, to the point. The work of democracy involves espousing those values that, in a less-democratic society, *would* get one sent to prison. To maintain its "sustainable edge," a democracy requires its citizens to actually risk something, to test the limits of the acceptable; the trajectory of capability building they must devote themselves to, above all others, is the one that advances the capability for making trouble. In sum, if the value you're espousing is one that could never get anyone, anywhere, sent to prison, then strictly democratically speaking, you're useless.

All of this helps explain why, in today's repressive societies, the sciences do not come in for the same treatment as the humanities. Not only are the sciences, with a few notable exceptions, politically neutral (there is no scientific equivalent of the samizdat pamphlet), their specialized languages tend to segregate them from the wider population, making ideological contagion difficult. More importantly, their work, quite often, is translatable into "product," which any aspiring dictatorship from Kazakhstan to Venezuela recognizes as an unambiguous good, whereas the

---

* Andrei Sakharov leaps to mind, though of course the roster of genuinely courageous, politically involved scientists is extensive.

work of the humanities—largely invisible, incremental at best, ideologically combustive—almost never is.

To put it simply, science addresses the outer world; the humanities, the inner one. Science explains how the material world is now for *all* men; the humanities, in their indirect, slippery way, offer the raw materials from which the individual constructs a self—a self *distinct* from others. The sciences, to push the point a bit, produce people who study things, and who can therefore, presumably, make or fix or improve these things; they are thus largely, though certainly not exclusively, an economic force.* The humanities offer a different product.

One might, then, reasonably expect the two, each invaluable in its own right, to operate on an equal footing in the United States, to receive equal attention and respect. Not so. In fact, not even close. From the *Sputnik*-inspired emphasis on "science and math" to the pronouncements of our recently retired "education president" (the jury is still out on Obama), the call is always for more investment in "math and science." And then a little more. The "American Competitiveness Initiative" calls for doubling federal spending on basic research grants in the physical sciences over ten years, at a cost of $50 billion. The federal government is asked to pay the cost of finding 30,000 math and science teachers. Senator Bill Frist pushes for grants for students majoring in math and science.

Whether the bias trickles down or percolates up, it's systemic. The New York City Department of Education announces housing incentives worth up to $15,000 to lure teachers "in math and science" to the city's schools. Classes in history and art and foreign

---

* As Don Randel, president of the Mellon Foundation, recently pointed out to me, part of the success of the sciences in the United States is due to the willingness of some in the scientific community to market themselves as a job-generating force despite the fact that the vast majority of scientific research conducted in America has, rightly, little or no economic utility.

languages are cut back to make room for their more practical, "rigorous" cousins. The Howard Hughes Medical Institute announces its selection of twenty new professors who will use their million-dollar grants to develop fresh approaches to teaching science. Nothing remotely comparable exists in the humanities.

Popular culture, meanwhile, plays backup, cementing bias into cliché. Mathandscience becomes the all-purpose marker for intelligence: it's cool, it's sexy, it has that all-American aura of money about it. Want to convey a character's intelligence? Show him solving equations on a napkin. Want to sex up homework, send a redeeming message to the kids? Make sure your romantic heroine (like Gabriella in *High School Musical 2*) gets As in math and science.

To appreciate how far the humanities have fallen, imagine Gabriella quoting *The Federalist Papers* or *Common Sense*. Imagine her, between dance numbers, immersed in Nietzsche's *The Atheist Viewpoint* or Robert Musil's *The Man Without Qualities*. It's nearly impossible; worse, it's weird. Clearly the girl's a troublemaker, one of those people who "have ideas," who are always complicating everything, who are never content to leave well enough alone. You say she gets "As in mathandscience"? Ah, now we get it. The kid's smart. She'll get a good job. She's on her way to a quality adult outcome.

State of Play

We want our students to grow up into people who are curious, teachable, and clear-minded. We want them to take into their interactions with others, into their readings, into their private thoughts, depth of experience and a willingness to be wrong. Only a study of the humanities provides that.

—MARCUS EURE, ENGLISH TEACHER, BREWSTER HIGH SCHOOL

No assessment of the marginalized role of the humanities today is possible without first admitting the complicity of those in the humanities themselves, myself included. Outmanned, outfunded, perpetually on the defensive, we have adapted to the hostile environment by embracing a number of survival strategies, among them camouflage, mimicry, and, altogether too effectively, playing dead. None of these is a strategy for success.

Which is not to say that the performance is without interest. Happily ignoring the fact that the whole point of reading is to force us into an encounter with the other, our high schools and colleges labor mightily to provide students with mirrors of their own experience, lest they be made uncomfortable, effectively undercutting diversity in the name of diversity. Some may actually believe in this. The rest, unable or unwilling to make the hard argument to parents and administrators, bend to the prevailing winds, shaping their curricula to appeal to the greatest number, a strategy suitable to advertising, not teaching.

Since it's not just the material itself but also what's done with it that can lead to trouble (even the most staid "classic," subjected to the right pressures by the right teacher, can yield its measure of discomfort), how we teach must be adjusted as well. Thus we encourage anemic discussions about Atticus Finch and racism but race past the boogeyman of miscegenation; thus we debate the legacy of the Founders, but tactfully sidestep their issues with Christianity; thus we teach *Walden*, if we teach it at all, as an ode to Nature, and ignore its full-frontal assault on the tenets of capitalism. Thus we tiptoe through the minefield, leaving the mines intact and loaded.

Still, the evasions and capitulations made by those on the secondary-school level are nothing compared to the tactics of their university counterparts, who, in a pathetic attempt to ape their more successful colleagues in the sciences, have developed their own faux-scientific, isolating jargon, effectively robbing themselves of their greatest virtue, their ability to influence (or infect) the general population. Self-erasure is rarely this effective, or ironic. Not content with trivializing itself through the subjects it considers important, nor with having assured its irrelevance by making itself unintelligible, the study of literature, for example, has taken its birthright and turned it into a fetish, that is, adopted the word *politics*—God, the irony!—and cycled it through so many levels of metaphorical interpretation that nothing recognizable remains except the husk. Politically neuter, we now sing the "politics" of oculocentric rhetoric. Safe in our tenured nests, we risk neither harm nor good.

If the self-portrait is unflattering, I can't apologize. Look at us! Look at how we've let the fashion for economic utility intimidate us, how we simultaneously cringe and justify ourselves, how we secretly despise the philistines, who could never understand the relevance of our theoretical flea circus, even as we rush, in a paroxysm of class guilt, to offer classes in Introductory Sit-Com Writing, in Clown 500, in *Seinfeld;* classes in which "everyone is a winner." Small wonder the sciences don't respect us; *we* shouldn't respect us.

And what have we gained from all this? Alas, despite our eagerness to fit in, to play ball, we *still* don't belong, we're still ignored or infantilized. What we've earned is the prerogative of going out with a whimper. Marginalized, self-righteous, we just keep on keeping on, insulted that no one returns our calls, secretly expecting no less.

Which makes it all the more impressive that there remain individuals who stubbornly hold the line, who either haven't noticed or don't care what's happened to the humanities in America, who daily fight for relevance, and achieve it. Editors, journalists, university and foundation presidents, college and high school teachers, they neither apologize nor equivocate nor retreat a single inch. Seen rightly, what could be more in the American grain?

Let the few stand for the many. Historian Drew Faust seems determined to use her bully pulpit as president of Harvard to call attention to the distorting force of our vocational obsession. Don Randel, president of the Mellon Foundation, the single largest supporter of the humanities in America, speaks of the humanities' unparalleled ability to force us into "a rigorous cross-examination of our myths about ourselves." Poet, classicist, and former dean of humanities at the University of Chicago Danielle Allen patiently advances the argument that the work of the humanities doesn't reveal itself within the typical three- or five-year cycle, that the humanities work on a fifty-year cycle, a hundred-year cycle.

Public high school English teacher Marcus Eure, meanwhile, teaching in the single most conservative county in New York State, labors daily "to dislocate the complacent mind," to teach students to parse not only *what* they are being told but *how* they are being told. His course in rhetoric—enough to give a foolish man hope—exposes the discrete parts of effective writing and reading, then nudges students to redefine their notion of "correct" to mean precise, logical, nuanced, and inclusive. His unit on lying asks students to read the "Yes, Virginia, there is a Santa Claus" letter from the *Sun* and Stephanie Ericsson's "The Ways We Lie," then consider how we define lying, whether we condone it under certain circumstances, how we learn to do it. "Having to treat Santa Claus as a systemic lie," Eure notes, "even if we can argue for its necessity, troubles a lot of them."

As does, deliberately, Eure's unit on torture, which uses Michael Levin's "The Case for Torture" to complicate the "us vs. them" argument, then asks students to consider Stephen King's "Why We Crave Horror Movies" and David Edelstein's article on "torture porn," "Now Playing at Your Local Multiplex." Inevitably, the question of morality comes up, as does the line between catharsis and desensitization. Eure allows the conversation to twist and complicate itself, to cut a channel to a video game called *The Sims*, which many of the students have played and in which most of them have casually killed the simulated human beings whose world they controlled. The students argue about what it means to watch a movie like *Saw*, what it means to live in a society that produces, markets, and supports such products.

Challenged to defend the utility of his classes, Eure asks his questioner to describe an American life in which the skills he is trying to inculcate are unnecessary. Invariably, he says, it becomes obvious that there is no such life, that *every* aspect of life—every marriage, every job, every parent-teacher meeting—hinges in some way on the ability to understand and empathize with others, to challenge one's beliefs, to strive for reason and clarity.

Muzzle the trumpets, still the drums. The market for reason is slipping fast. The currency of unreason and demagoguery is daily gathering strength. The billboards in the Panhandle proclaim "God, Guns and Guts Made America Free." Today, the Marcus Eures of America resemble nothing so much as an island ecosystem, surrounded by the times. Like that ecosystem, they are difficult, unamenable, and necessary, and, also like that ecosystem, their full value may not be fully understood until they've disappeared, forcing us into a bankruptcy none of us wish to contemplate.

Perhaps there's still time to reinstate the qualifier to its glory, to invest our capital in what makes us human.

Acknowledgments

Though I am wary of institutional loyalty, in this instance, an exception is in order. Many of these essays first appeared in *Harper's Magazine*, and I am deeply grateful to that prickly, irreverent, essential publication for regularly providing me with a brass trumpet and a lot of rope; that I have managed to make a little noise without hanging myself conclusively is largely due to the diligence of a number of individuals there, primarily Ben Metcalf and Colin Harrison, whom I thank for their guidance and their kindness. May the magazine that has supported us all, that first appeared a year before *Moby-Dick* was published, continue, unbowed, for another 150 years.

Of the many personal debts incurred, I want to single out my debt to Sacvan Bercovitch. At times, in these essays, I've drafted off his brilliant work in American literature and culture, just as, in a larger sense, I've drafted, these thirty-five years, off his fascination with the world, his nose for the absurd, his humor, his grace.

Photo: Maya Slouka

Mark Slouka is the author of a collection of stories, *Lost Lake;* a book of nonfiction, *War of the Worlds;* and two novels, *God's Fool* and *The Visible World.* A contributing editor to *Harper's Magazine,* he lives with his wife and children outside of New York City.

Book design by Rachel Holscher. Composition by BookMobile Design and Publishing Services, Minneapolis, Minnesota. Manufactured by Versa Press on acid-free paper.